SUBSTANCE ABUSE AND GANG VIOLENCE

OTHER RECENT VOLUMES IN THE
SAGE FOCUS EDITIONS

SUBSTANCE ABUSE
AND
GANG VIOLENCE

Richard C. Cervantes
editor

SAGE PUBLICATIONS
International Educational and Professional Publisher
Newbury Park   London   New Delhi

For information address:

SAGE Publications, Inc.
2455 Teller Road
Newbury Park, California 91320

SAGE Publications Ltd.
6 Bonhill Street
London EC2A 4PU
United Kingdom

SAGE Publications India Pvt. Ltd.
M-32 Market
Greater Kailash I
New Delhi 110 048 India

Printed in the United States of America

Library of Congress Cataloging-in-Publication Data

Main entry under title:

Substance abuse and gang violence / edited by Richard C. Cervantes.
        p. cm. — (Sage focus editions: 147)
    Includes bibliographical references and index.
    ISBN 0-8039-4283-4 (cl). — ISBN 0-8039-4284-2 (pb)
    1. Gangs—United States. 2. Narcotics and crimes—United States.
    3. Violence—United States.   I. Cervantes, Richard C.
    HV6439.U5S83   1992
    364.2'4—dc20   92-20226

92 93 94 95   10 9   8   7   6   5   4   3   2   1

Sage Production Editor: Judith L. Hunter

Contents

Preface

Gangs, violence, drug and alcohol abuse—these subjects have become increasingly prominent in the public's eyes. Research in the past has noted the increase in drug use and abuse within gangs as well as in the general population. Paramount among the reasons cited by researchers for the spread of substance abuse are personal stresses stemming from environmental pressures such as breakdowns in the family, joblessness, and culture conflict. To exacerbate the problems associated with substance abuse, the upsurge in illicit drug sales and trafficking has made drugs more commonly available. While alcohol has long been widely available and widely abused, only small segments of the American population experienced illicit drug abuse. Now, it is so widespread that even young children are exposed to these substances. In the past two decades, new substances such as PCP and "rock" cocaine have been added to what is now a literal smorgasbord of drugs available to users.

This book is an attempt to address some of the important issues revolving around gangs and gang members' drug habits, particularly the relationships they have with gang violence. Research, policy and legal issues, prevention strategies, and victims of violence comprise the topical categories include in this volume. In this respect, the editor and the authors recognize that the issue of gangs, drugs, and violence is multifaceted and requires different approaches if we are going to understand and effectively strive toward dealing with it.

The richness of the content here is more than matched by the diversity of the authors, in both their varied experiences and their perspectives. They range from local to national governmental officials. Some are university-based while others work in community service agencies, health services, and law enforcement. Recent developments indicate that the problem of gangs and drug use/abuse is going to require more than just one solution. Indeed, as I have noted elsewhere, there are multiple strands to this complex issue which will necessitate the use of a number of different coordinated prevention and intervention strategies.

In the research section of the book, the clear message is that important similarities exist in the phenomenon of gang violence and substance abuse. However, caution also must be taken to consider the important local, regional, and specific ethnic variations in these patterns. For example, the specific relationships between drug trafficking and gang violence contrast greatly across the broad ethnic categories, and there is diversity as well within the intra-ethnic categories, such as that found among Asian Americans. Such variations are also characteristic of substance abuse patterns and levels of gang violence.

In the past 15 years or so, law enforcement has been overburdened with virtually sole responsibility for a solution to both gang violence and drug problems. The initial enthusiasm on the part of law enforcement has waned as it has became clear that no amount of police suppression can of itself adequately address these problems. In part, in fact, these very efforts at police suppression have helped bring about the spread of drug-related gang activities into areas where they were previously nonexistent, as drug traffickers relocated some of their illicit trade from heavily policed urban areas to less well patrolled neighborhoods.

Prevention strategies are now widely recognized as a required complement to police efforts to address substance abuse and gang violence. More and more experts are suggesting that these issues constitute a public health problem. As with many public health problems this one originates and grows in conditions of urban poverty, neighborhood decay, stressed families, and, in short, the myriad characteristics found in the city's ethnic minority underclass population. As with other public health problems, also, drug-related gang activities eventually—if not adequately addressed—will spread beyond the boundaries of those communities to infect the public at large. This fact necessitates levels of preventive strategies designed to address the various facets of the problem. Schools, courts, and the community at large, for example, must play specific roles in developing and effecting prevention policies.

The devastating effects of gang violence go beyond the primary victim, as untold hardships accrue to the loved ones and the many other community members who are also made to suffer. Thus, the ripple effects of gang violence and drug abuse, including overdose, magnify the already severe problems affecting poor minority neighborhoods, and are now spreading into other neighborhoods. As we approach the twenty-first century simple, single-faceted efforts to deal with the rising gang violence problem and the substance abuse associated with it must undergo a rethinking by researchers and policy analysts. Failure to arrive at more viable solutions to the problem will increasingly make victims of us all. The authors presented in this volume remind us of the complexity of the problem facing us, as well as the dangers of not facing up to it.

—JAMES DIEGO VIGIL

Introduction

The gang phenomenon has been documented and studied by social scientists for nearly a century. Refined and expanded theories have emerged to help guide our research methods, our prevention and intervention approaches. Perhaps at no other time in history, however, has a systematic, multilevel, and well-grounded understanding of gangs been more needed. The toll on individual lives, families, and communities that results from gang-related violence is hard to measure, but by all counts has reached epidemic proportions. Closely linked to the gang phenomenon is the sale, use, and abuse of various illicit substances, as well as alcohol. Large profits from the sale of these illicit substances provide an important source of economic stimulation in communities that otherwise are mere skeletons of urban life. The frame of reference for many youths (and families) residing in such impoverished social and economic conditions is so limited that gang membership becomes valued. The immediate effects of drug use at the individual level greatly impair judgment and reasoning, and likely only serve to lower inhibitions toward violent acting out.

In March of 1990 a national conference to articulate issues of and solutions to the substance abuse and gang violence problem was held in Los Angeles, California. The conference, The National Conference on Substance Abuse and Gang Violence, sponsored by the U.S. Office for Substance Abuse Prevention (OSAP) (Alcohol, Drug and Mental Health Administration Grant No. H13 SP01642-01) was organized around the concept that a multidisciplinary approach would be needed to begin addressing such a complex social (and economic) issue. Specific papers from this conference were selected for this publication, again with a multidisciplinary perspective in mind.

As the reader will see, these chapters have been developed by research scholars, law enforcement specialists, educators, and mental health professionals, and cover a rather wide spectrum of issues. It is hoped that this edited book will serve as a source of information for others who are dedicated to the scientific study of youths, as well those who provide prevention and other human services to youths who may be at particular risk for becoming victims or perpetrators of gang-related violence.

The editor would especially like to thank Sergio Castillo and Tia Hoffer for their insight in the review process, as well as Kristine Stokes for her many hours of effort in the preparation of the book. Finally, the editor would like to thank the administration and staff of the California School of Professional Psychology, Los Angeles, for their support in the original conference coordination and subsequent preparation of the book.

—RICHARD C. CERVANTES

PART I

Research Issues

1

Substance Abuse Among Asian/Pacific Islander Americans

TOSHIAKI SASAO

Introduction

Despite the increasing diversity of Asian/Pacific Islanders (A/PI) in the United States (Asian Week, Inc., 1991; U.S. General Accounting Office, 1990), reliable empirical data on the epidemiology of alcohol and other drug (AOD) use among various A/PI groups are sorely lacking (Zane & Sasao, in press). This is unfortunate because this paucity of data on AOD use tends to reinforce the myth that Asians are the "model minority" and free from significant social problems including AOD use, AIDS, gang and family violence, child abuse, and unemployment. As a consequence, AOD service needs are often neglected for the A/PI communities.

This chapter will discuss the current patterns and extent of substance abuse among A/PI Americans by providing a critical review of what little information exists in the empirical research literature. Some conceptual and methodological issues that may contribute to the difficulties in estimating the prevalence of substance abuse among Asian/Pacific Islanders will also be discussed. Such discussion may prove useful for advancing research on substance abuse within the larger context of Asian-American health and mental health. Finally, findings from the recently conducted

AUTHOR'S NOTE: The preparation of the manuscript was in part supported by a grant from the California Department of Alcohol and Drug Programs (#D-0008-9). Helpful comments by Richard Cervantes on an earlier draft of the chapter are greatly appreciated.

3

statewide needs assessment project (Sasao, 1991a) on Asian AOD problems in California will be presented with implications for future research directions.

Extent of Alcohol and Other Drug Use/Abuse
Among Asian/Pacific Islander Americans: A Critical Review

The empirical research literature provides mixed findings about the nature and extent of AOD problems among A/PI populations. For instance, a number of survey studies have found that Asian/Pacific Islanders do not seem to use or abuse substances as frequently as other non-Asian groups (see Austin, Prendergast & Lee, 1989; Johnson & Nishi, 1976; Trimble, Padilla, & Bell, 1987; Zane & Sasao, in press, for literature review). In contrast, clinical and anecdotal evidence suggests that serious substance abuse problems exist for certain Asian/Pacific populations (e.g., Nakashima, 1986). Thus, there is an obvious need for more empirical work on Asian/Pacifics that can facilitate effective prevention and treatment of AOD problems in these communities.

An examination of the empirical literature on AOD use among A/PI groups reveals that there are a very few methodologically sound studies that directly investigate the problem. Some of the methodological problems include: (a) exclusive focus on the larger and more accultu-rated Asian groups, such as Chinese and Japanese; (b) use of mainly student samples; (c) inaccessibility to Asian groups who may be at greatest risk for substance abuse problems (e.g., refugees, recent immi-grants, adolescents); (d) use of disproportionately small sample sizes; (e) socioeconomic and other demographic differences, seldom being controlled, that may be confounded with ethnicity; (f) failure to use bilingual measures without evaluating conceptual equivalence; (g) fail-ure to account for cultural differences that may affect self-report or self-disclosure with respect to AOD use and abuse. Given these meth-odological problems, extreme caution is required in interpreting some of the research findings.

To facilitate the literature review below, two categories of research were identified according to the type of populations used: (a) those research studies that used untreated cases in the general community or student samples; and (b) those research studies that examined treated cases including either existing archival data bases and/or clinical cases observed at drug treatment facilities.

Estimates From Untreated Cases

Much of the evidence for infrequent abuse or relatively lower use of substances among Asians has been documented in research using surveys of untreated cases from community or student samples. Most studies have compared various ethnic groups, but specific Asian subgroups have not been identified or differentiated, thus making it difficult to determine if the findings can truly be generalized to the various Asian/Pacific Islander populations.

In a study comparing Asian, primarily American-born Chinese and Japanese, with non-Asian students at the University of Washington, Sue, Zane, and Ito (1979) found that Asian students consumed less alcohol, had more negative attitudes toward drinking, and used fewer cues in the regulation of their own drinking than non-Asian counterparts. It was suggested that with assimilation into American culture came more lenient and positive attitudes toward alcohol consumption, including the possibility of alcohol abuse.

Several more recent student surveys (Maddahian, Newcomb, & Bentler, 1985, 1986; McCarthy, Newcomb, Maddahian, & Skager, 1986; Newcomb, Maddahian, Skager, & Bentler, 1987) also have revealed that the Asian respondents in California tend to report lower levels of substance use in terms of cigarettes, alcohol, marijuana, cocaine, and other hard drugs when compared to other ethnic groups, particularly Caucasians. For example, in the Newcomb and colleagues (1987) study, data were collected anonymously in 1985 from 2,926 7th, 9th, and 11th graders in Ventura County, California. The study assessed substance abuse frequency, perceived harmfulness of marijuana, perceived parental attitudes toward drug use, and mood state measures. When the risk factors (e.g., emotional distress, educational aspirations, and psychological adjustment) were constructed for different groups, the Asians also showed the lowest level of risk for future substance abuse. As with other studies, the small sample size of Asians ($n = 77$) limits the generalizability of the findings because the study excluded many sociocultural variables important for examining individual differences among A/PI Americans (e.g., acculturation level, family relationships, peer relationships).

Adlaf, Smart, and Tan (1989) compared drug use patterns across eight ethnic groups in Ontario, Canada. This study sought to examine inter-ethnic differences, but their operationalization of ethnicity varied from other studies. Ethnic group affiliation was designated as the ethnicity of participants' "ancestors on the male side on coming to this continent." Judged by this definition, presumably participants of mixed ethnicity were included in the various ethnic samples. After controlling for certain demographic variables such as level of acculturation, religion, age, provincial region, and gender, the Asian group (Chinese and Japanese combined, $n = 102$) had the lowest use of tobacco, alcohol, and cannabis.

Thus, the previous studies appear to present convergent evidence of relatively lower substance use among Asians from different geographical regions. However, these comparisons with other ethnic groups may be difficult to interpret because the Asian sample sizes were extremely small in both an absolute and a relative sense. In each ethnic comparison of this study, the Asian or Asian/ Pacific group constituted less than 3% of the total survey sample. The actual number of respondents studied ranged from 63 to 117.

The few studies that have included sizeable samples of Asians have been conducted in either California or Hawaii. Two studies conducted in Los Angeles on seventh and eighth graders (Projects SMART & SHARP, John Graham, Ph.D., University of Southern California, personal communication, 1988) indicated that the lifetime use of cigarettes, marijuana, and alcohol was lower for Asian/Pacifics compared to blacks, Hispanics, or Caucasians. Similar patterns of use were found in a statewide survey of drug and alcohol use among students in grades 7, 9, and 11 (Skager, Frith, & Maddahian, 1986, 1989). One of the few studies to examine inter-Asian differences in substance use was conducted as part of a statewide alcohol, drug, and mental health epidemiological survey in the state of Hawaii (Johnson, Nagoshi, Ahern, Wilson, & Yuen, 1987; McLaughlin, Raymond, Murakami, & Gilbert, 1987). Using a face-to-face interview with both Asians and non-Asians, researchers determined the relative prevalence of alcohol and other drug use among Chinese Americans, Japanese Americans, Filipino Americans, Native Hawaiians, and Caucasians. Results of the survey revealed that Native Hawaiians and Caucasians reported a higher level of use for all drugs, with the exception of tranquilizers, when compared to the three Asian groups. However, Asian groups (Chinese, Japanese, and Filipino) appear to use tranquilizers, marijuana/hashish, and pain drugs as frequently or more than non-Asian groups. Interestingly, although the use of alcohol has been reported to be very prevalent among A/PI communities, alcohol was cited far less frequently by all Asian groups compared to non-Asian groups. It appears that certain cultural factors may be operating whereby Asian/Pacific Americans are using alcohol and drugs primarily for self-medication purposes to alleviate depression, pain, and other socially acceptable physical illnesses, but not for recreational purposes. While the results underscore the importance of examining inter-Asian differences in substance use, it is unclear if the actual differences found can be generalized to non-Hawaiian A/PI communities on the mainland. A number of investigators have noted how Hawaiian Asian groups may be quite different from their mainland counterparts in terms of their non-minority status, acculturation, English language proficiency, community cohesiveness, social-political identification, and so on (Kitano & Daniels, 1988; Sue & Morishima, 1982). Thus, there is a need to replicate their findings with mainland A/PIs before any definitive statement can be made about such prevalence data.

A bilingual telephone survey (n = 127) of a predominantly Japanese community in Southern California was conducted to assess not only the community's perception of substance abuse prevalence but also the community members' own use of cigarettes, alcohol, and marijuana (Sasao, 1991b). The results indicated that substance abuse is perceived as a significant social issue in this community. Respondents reported the levels of lifetime alcohol use (73%) and cigarette use (55%), which are slightly lower than the levels of the general American public (85% lifetime alcohol and 75% lifetime cigarette use among those who are 12 years old or older), according to the *1988 National Household Survey on Drug Abuse* (National Institute on Drug Abuse, 1990). Further analysis of 30-day prevalence revealed that 55% of all lifetime cigarettes users and 61% of all lifetime alcohol users had used the substance in the past month. In the past, using the telephone as a mode of data collection has been criticized with respect to the biased sampling due to low survey cooperation, reliability/validity problems, and anonymity/ confidentiality issues. However, in this phone survey the rate of interview completion was high (82%). Important differences occurred between American-born and Japanese-born respondents. Compared to the former, the latter had a higher rate of refusing to participate and exhibited less knowledge and social concern over AOD use or abuse. The majority of the Japanese-born respondents were housewives of Japanese businessmen, who tended to reside in the United States for only a short period of time. There also appeared to be a difference in the manner by which the two subgroups defined "substance abuse." The Japanese-born respondents tended to reserve this term for only for such hard drugs as marijuana, LSD, and heroin, and did not include alcohol use and cigarette use as potential substance abuse problems. The American-born definition of substance abuse was more inclusive, involving the use of alcohol and cigarettes. This difference may have important implications for prevention work with Japanese of different generations.

In a number of studies focused only on alcohol drinking patterns among Asians, Harry Kitano and his colleagues at UCLA questioned the myth of Asian/Pacific Americans as non-drinkers (Kitano & Chi, 1985; Kitano, Lubben & Chi, 1988; Lubben, Chi, & Kitano, 1989). Surnames of Chinese, Japanese, and Korean respondents were drawn from Los Angeles phone directories, in proportion to the Los Angeles population of each group. For the Filipino respondents, the "snowball" sampling technique was used: Initial interviews with Filipinos from known organizations were followed by referral to other potential Filipino subjects. The final sample included 298 Chinese, 295 Japanese, 280 Koreans, and 230 Filipinos. The demographic characteristics indicated that most of these respondents were married men between the ages of 30 and 60.

Results indicated that the alcohol drinking pattern of young Asian males is very similar to that found for a national sample of young adult male respondents (Cahalan & Cisin, 1976) and that certain Asian groups had a high proportion of heavy drinkers. The Japanese (25.4%) and Filipinos (19.6%) had the highest percentage of heavy drinkers, followed by the Koreans (14.6%) and the Chinese (10.4%). Analyses of attitude items corroborated the findings of Sue and colleagues (1979), in which more permissive attitudes associated with greater acculturation were related to heavier alcohol consumption. It appears, then, that at least in the case of alcohol consumption, Asian substance use has been underestimated. In a related finding, Maddahian and colleagues (1985) found that Asians were the largest group that tried only alcohol and no other substances. Kitano has explained that the diversity and variability among various Asians in their drinking patterns can be attributed to the cultural patterns brought over by their ancestors. This study was one of the first large sample surveys conducted to determine the alcohol drinking practices of various A/PI groups. However, the sampling methodology, which involved household interviews based on the phone directories and the snowball technique, may have omitted certain individuals in the Asian population considered at highest risk for alcohol problems (e.g., single, recently emigrated males living alone or in crowded communal arrangements with no private telephones).

Another large epidemiological survey of alcohol use among Chinese, Japanese, Caucasians, and Asian-Caucasians (mixed parentage) was conducted in Hawaii (Murakami, 1989). This survey was designed to control for the effects of certain sociodemographic variables (e.g., social class, gender, marital status). Caucasians tended to drink more and flush less than either the Chinese or the Japanese, whereas the two Asian groups did not differ from one another in drinking or flushing. Individuals of mixed Asian-Caucasian ancestry had mean alcohol consumption levels that were very similar to those of the Caucasian group and considerably higher than those of the Asian groups. However, Asian-Caucasians resembled Asians more than Caucasians in their tendency to flush. Results suggest that cultural variables such as assimilation (in this case, marital assimilation) into American mainstream culture have an important influence on the extent of alcohol use.

Given the diversity of the Asian/Pacific population in this country, it would be especially important to examine the substance use patterns of Asian/Pacific groups considered at high risk for health and/or mental health problems. Yee and Thu (1987) reported on the prevalence and nature of the substance use problems among one such group, the Indochinese refugees. Their study sampled 840 Indochinese refugees, mainly Vietnamese, residing in Houston, Texas, and several cities in Louisiana, and employed household interviews to assess AOD use and mental health status. Approximately 45% of the sample reported problems involving drinking alcohol and/or tobacco use, although the use of other drugs was not seen as problematic. A significant number of respondents viewed alcohol and smoking as acceptable ways both for directly coping with stressful situations and for alleviating personal problems resulting from stress.

Wong (1985) investigated the substance abuse among Chinese youth in a community associated with high-risk indicators, San Francisco's Chinatown. Using a non-random sampling of 123 Chinese youths, ages 13 to 19, Wong estimated that the prevalence of substance abuse among these youth was *higher* than that found among other youth in the previous study conducted in San Francisco with the same methodology. The lifetime use of cigarettes, marijuana, cocaine, and Valium in the Chinese sample was similar to that reported by the non-Asian samples (Caucasians, blacks, Hispanics). The Chinese sample tended to use Quaaludes more frequently than the other groups.

Estimates From Treated Cases

The use of treated cases or utilization data to estimate prevalence is a hazardous venture fraught with selection biases due to socioeconomic, administrative, and other nosocomial factors (Kramer & Zane, 1984). Nevertheless, this approach provides an alternative source for examining Asian substance use and abuse.

In recent years, in both San Francisco and Los Angeles, Asian/Pacifics using drug abuse treatment services have been consistently under-represented with respect to their respective proportions in the local populations. This has commonly been interpreted as reflecting service under-utilization (Murase, 1977) rather than a lesser need for services related to lower levels of AOD use.

Asian, Inc. (1978) used a key informant approach and estimated that the substance use of Chinese and Filipinos is lower than that of the general population, whereas the level of use for Japanese is similar to that found in the general San Francisco population. In a national study of drug abuse programs, Phin and Phillips (1978) found that A/PIs (55%) and Caucasians (63%-67%) were primarily admitted for heroin abuse. As for drug abuse patterns, A/PIs relative to Caucasians indicated a greater involvement with barbiturates (45% and 11%, respectively). Using the information collected from a large ambulatory population under the care of the Kaiser-Permanente Medical Care Program in its Oakland and San Francisco facilities, Klatsky, Friedman, Siegelaub, and Gerard (1977) reported that when compared to Whites, Blacks, and Others, Asian/Pacific males and females ($n = 4,319$), under a generic category "Yellow," had the highest level of abstinence from alcohol. Namkung (1976) found that of the A/PIs in the California prison population, 95% were incarcerated for drug-related reasons. These studies have suffered from the same limitations as the untreated cases studies by not distinguishing between different Asian groups, using relatively small samples, not controlling for important demographic variations, and assuming cultural equivalence among the self-report measures and interview procedures.

The State of California has one of the largest databases of treated cases, the California Drug Abuse Data System (CAL-DADS),[1] which many local agencies and government use to make policy decisions. This database replaced the Client Oriented Data Acquisition Process (CODAP) System on July 1, 1982, when the National Institute on Drug Abuse discontinued its system. Information for CAL-DADS is collected by clinics that use state or federal funds to provide direct treatment services to drug abuse clients. Some of the data include demographic characteristics, drug abuse patterns, and treatment summaries for each client.

The CAL-DADS admission data for Los Angeles and San Francisco counties indicate that the use of drugs (mainly heroin, marijuana, and cocaine) had been fairly stable from 1982 to 1989 (Sasao, 1990). Asian/Pacific Islanders had the lowest admission rates to county or federal treatment facilities. Again, this appears to reflect under-utilization rather than a lower need for services on the part of A/PI populations.

Summary

Research on either untreated or treated cases has produced a mixed pattern of findings in estimating the level of substance use among Asian/Pacifics. Nevertheless, certain tentative conclusions can be formed. First, it appears that alcohol use has been underestimated, particularly for certain Asian groups, such as Japanese and Filipino males. Second, there is some evidence that suggests that a major substance abuse problem for older Asian groups may involve the use of barbiturates, tranquilizers, and pain drugs. Third, cultural factors appear to play an important role in limiting and, at other times, enhancing substance use among certain Asian groups. Fourth, the past research has not been very informative because it is usually unclear which Asian groups are being studied. This is a serious methodological shortcoming because the Asian groups that appear at highest risk for developing substance abuse problems either have seldom been studied or have not been separately identified in previous research. Finally, it is highly likely that the estimates provided by these data will soon be outdated and grossly underestimated because many of the groups with the highest risk factors (i.e., Southeast Asian refugees, Koreans, and Filipinos) are the fastest growing groups in the Asian population. Whereas the Japanese and Chinese constituted the largest groups in 1970, it is estimated that by the year 2000 the Filipinos will be largest group, followed by the Chinese, Vietnamese, Koreans, and Japanese. Thus, as significant changes in socio-demographic and ethnic profile of the general Asian/Pacific population occur, these undoubtedly will be associated with certain changes in AOD use and abuse patterns.

Statewide Asian Drug Abuse Needs Assessment in California: A Multimethod Approach

As it was made clear earlier, relying on one single method in addressing the epidemiology of AOD use or abuse among the A/PI population is inadequate and misleading because of many methodological and conceptual issues that need to be addressed. A single approach or method, when used by itself, runs a high risk of estimation error (Brewer & Hunter, 1989; Campbell & Fiske, 1959; Denzin, 1970; Riley, Wagenfeld, & Sonnard, 1981; Sasao, in preparation). Thus, in our needs assessment, we used a multimethod approach in which various methods were utilized in order to find convergence in determining prevalence and other service needs in Asian/Pacific Islander communities.

Each of the following four methods provided the basis for the estimation of AOD prevalence and service needs among the diverse and growing communities of A/PI descent from different perspectives:[2] (1) Community Telephone Survey (general community residents' perspectives); (2) Community Forums/Client Focus Groups (perspectives of local community leaders and current/ex-AOD users); (3) AOD Use Indicator (Archival Data) Study (administrators/policymakers' perspectives); and (4) Service Utilization Study (administrators/policymakers' perspectives). The findings of this needs assessment are fully described elsewhere (Sasao, 1991a).

Methodology and Major Findings

Community Phone Survey

In the community telephone survey, a total of 1,783 community residents in Chinese ($n = 409$), Japanese ($n = 416$), Korean ($n = 399$), Filipino ($n = 159$), and Vietnamese (including ethnic Chinese) ($n = 400$) in Northern and Southern California were interviewed in order to collect information on the prevalence of AOD use/abuse and other drug-related problems, including social psychological correlates. Although the response rates and refusal rates varied considerably from group to group (response rates ranging from 31% to 67%; and refusal rates, from 8% to 46%), the final respondents represented wide geographical regions in the state of California (see Sasao, 1991a, for a detailed description of sampling procedures). Results indicated that about 60% to 80% of the community residents in each ethnic group perceived that AOD use/abuse was a serious or moderately serious problem in their respective community. Alcohol and cigarettes were perceived to be the most commonly available substances in all Asian groups. Across all groups, self-reported lifetime use of marijuana and cocaine was generally low; however, issues of response biases need to be considered in interpreting these low prevalence rates. An interesting finding about personal use of alcohol and tobacco products is that more established groups, such as Japanese and Chinese, indicated *more* lifetime usage but *less* use in the past month; whereas newer immigrant groups, such as Vietnamese, Koreans, and Filipinos, indicated *more* use in the past month but *less* lifetime use. This indicates that use of alcohol and tobacco products, including cigarettes, seems to be rising in the latter groups, whereas its use among Japanese and Chinese appears stable.

Community Forums/Client Focus Groups

To collect qualitative, ethnographic information on the perceptions and attitudes of the local Asian community members regarding AOD use, and to procure suggestions for AOD prevention, 23 community forums and 18 client focus groups[3] were held in the greater San Francisco, Los Angeles, and San Diego areas. Unlike the focus of the Community Telephone Survey, the information collected via these community group discussions provided the perspectives from the service providers and the AOD users in local communities.

A community forum group discussion, ranging from 5 to 19 participants, was held in each local ethnic community. In each forum, a variety of community groups and organizations was represented, including social/mental health/health services, religious leaders, political groups, citizens groups, teachers and students, businesses, law enforcement personnel, AOD program staff, and religious organizations.

Community forum participants agreed that alcohol and tobacco products were used most frequently in all groups represented. The use of hard drugs such as marijuana and cocaine, including crack cocaine, was noted as "on the rise," especially among the new immigrant youth.

Eighteen client focus groups, consisting of 5 to 10 current and former AOD users in each, were held in the San Francisco, Los Angeles, and San Diego areas. Potential participants were first identified by local community contacts, such as AOD program staff and law enforcement staff. Those who agreed to participate in the discussion groups were asked to read and sign an informed consent form, and were also asked to refer us to other potential participants. Both females and males, with ages ranging from 16 to 60, were represented in each focus group.

Again, the focus group participants cited alcohol and tobacco products as the most frequently abused substances within most of the Asian communities. Also, cocaine and marijuana use was very common among many immigrant youths. It was noted that the seemingly low prevalence of hard drugs among Asians could be attributed to the fact that the Asian AOD users and their families usually deny or hide their AOD problems until the problems become out of control.

One major problem with qualitative data collected via these discussion groups is the possibility that those sampled do not constitute a representative sample of the targeted community. In an attempt to circumvent this problem, an extensive feedback process was implemented with each community studied. Each forum or focus group participant was given the opportunity to respond to preliminary reports of the group discussions. This feedback process not only served as a check on the report's accuracy but also established a systematic means through which community members, including service providers and AOD users, provided additional information to the needs assessment during the course of the study.

AOD Use Indicators (Archival Data) Study

Studying the indicators of AOD use/abuse is an effective methodology for monitoring AOD trends and patterns, and also for assessing the extent of the local AOD problem (NIDA, 1980; Robins, 1985).

Thus, four types of AOD use/abuse indicators, broken down by sex, age, and ethnicity, from several different sources (e.g., education, health, and drug treatment services) were collected for 15 counties in California where large numbers of Asian Pacific Islander populations reside, according to the preliminary release of 1990 U.S. Census information (Jerry Wong, U.S. Census Bureau, Department of Commerce, personal communication, November 1990). These indicators were:[4] (1) AIDS incidence, (2) drug-related deaths, (3) drug law violation arrests, and (4) school dropout rates.

(1) AIDS incidence. Acquired immune deficiency syndrome (AIDS) is commonly transmitted through the sharing of unsterile syringes by intravenous (IV) drug users; thus, the incidence of AIDS cases may be correlated with the prevalence of IV drug use (Siegel, 1988). The data were obtained from AIDS Surveillance Reports and AIDS Surveillance Programs from California counties. Analyses indicated that the percent-

age of A/PIs contracting the virus through IV drug use is the lowest among all ethnic groups, reflecting seemingly lower rates of heavy IV use among A/PI communities. However, given that AIDS is a highly stigmatizing disease and Asians are less likely to report having the disease, the numbers may be underestimated (Aoki, Ngin, Mo, & Ja, 1989).

(2) Drug-related deaths. The number of drug-related deaths is most useful for monitoring general patterns because an increase would indicate an increase in the number of self-administering, active heroin and other drug users. Analyses of data from the California State Department of Health Services indicated that the statewide percentage of Asian mortality (1985-1988) due to alcohol and drug-related causes was approximately 2%, which is far lower than that for the other ethnic groups. Suicide was the leading cause of such death, followed by poisoning and cocaine use. Similar analyses at the county level yielded too few cases in each cell for any meaningful analysis.

(3) Drug law violation arrests. The number of drug arrests is considered to reflect overall drug usage on the local level. The statewide data of felony and misdemeanor drug offenses by ethnicity for 1988 showed that the total number of Asians (Chinese, Japanese, and Filipinos) and Pacific Islanders combined composed only 0.3% of the total number of Californians arrested for drug offenses. Although this is an extremely low number, given that the estimated A/PI population in California is 10% according to the 1990 U.S. Census, it is notable that more Filipinos and Pacific Islanders are arrested for drug charges. In most counties, the number of A/PIs arrested was too minuscule to perform separate analyses.

(4) School dropout rates. Although youths drop out of public school systems for a number of reasons, it has been documented that AOD use or abuse accounts for a high number of dropouts among recent immigrant youths (Gregory Austin, Ph.D., Southwest Regional Laboratory, Los Alamitos, California, personal communication, November 18, 1991). Thus, as an indirect measure of possible AOD use, the school dropout rates may indicate AOD use among youth. Examination of school dropout rates obtained from the California State Department of Education, County and District Offices, revealed that the dropout rate for Asians (excluding Filipinos and Pacific Islanders) is lower than that for any other ethnic groups. However, the dropout rates for Pacific Islanders and Filipinos were among the highest. Therefore, it may be speculated that Filipino and Pacific Islander youths have been exposed to AOD use or abuse more often than the other groups because these

dropout youths are often found among gang members involving serious drug trafficking and abuse (Ernie Takemoto, Los Angeles County Probation Department, personal communication, September 6, 1991).

The AOD abuse/use indicator study is limited in generalizability of its conclusions that can be drawn because the data are indirect measures of AOD use/abuse. In many cases, data are not available for specific Asian ethnic groups, often categorized simply as "Asian," "Asian/Pacific Islanders," or "Other." Clearly, there is a need for many of the data sources to collect more accurate and detailed demographic and ethnic information.

Service Utilization Study

By examining trends in utilization of mental health and drug abuse treatment services, the patterns of AOD use or abuse among A/PI populations can be monitored. To this end, three data sets were analyzed: (a) Los Angeles County Mental Health System Data, (b) San Francisco City & County Mental Health System Data, and (c) California Drug Abuse Data System (CAL-DADS).

The Los Angeles County Mental Health System data set is a compilation of all client records for those who have entered public and private mental health service facilities in Los Angeles County since 1973. The present analyses for a 6-year period from 1982 to 1988 included all Asian clients (Chinese, Japanese, Filipino, Korean, Indochinese, and Other A/PIs) and matched samples of Caucasians, blacks, and Hispanics who met primary or secondary DSM-III or DSM-III-R diagnoses of psychoactive substance-induced organic mental disorders, withdrawal delirium, hallucinosis, amnestic disorder, and psychoactive substance use disorders. An analysis of the numbers of clients seeking treatment indicated that there were no notable trends from year to year in service utilization for A/PI clients. Due to small numbers of clients in each cell when broken down by year, ethnicity, and treatment setting, such analyses did not yield useful data in examining the pattern of treatment admissions for A/PIs in Los Angeles County. Ethnic comparison in service utilization showed that A/PIs utilized the mental health system less frequently than other ethnic groups. This should not be interpreted simply to mean that there is a lower frequency of serious drug problems that require treatment. Because treatment admission data serve only as an indirect indicator of AOD use or abuse in the mental health system, the findings found should be tempered further by the fact that many mental health service settings are not equipped to treat AOD cases. Analyses of the San Francisco Mental Health System Data, similarly organized and maintained as the Los Angeles System, indicated that in the 3-year period (1988 through 1990), there were no significant trends of AOD use patterns in any of the ethnic groups (Asians, blacks, Hispanics, and Caucasians). However, there appeared to be a severe under-utilization of services by Chinese, Japanese, or Filipino clients seeking drug treatment through the mental health system.

The CAL-DADS, noted earlier in the chapter, was used to assess the yearly trends of treatment admissions from 1982 to 1988 by ethnicity and drug types used. Across the counties and all ethnic groups, including Asians, heroin was by far the drug involved in the most treatment admissions. Although there appeared no significant overall annual trends, the frequency of those Asians seeking treatment shows slight trends for specific drugs in specific counties. For example, in Los Angeles County, admissions among all ethnic groups for cocaine abuse increased from 1982 to 1988, while admissions for marijuana and other drug use declined. In Orange County, the overall rise in the Asians' use of drug abuse treatment seems to be due largely to those seeking treatment for heroin use.

AOD Use and Abuse in Asian Pacific/Islander Communities in California: Another Myth or Reality?

The 1990 California Statewide Asian Drug Abuse Needs Assessment (Sasao, 1991a) was initiated in response to the lack of definitive data on the epidemiology of AOD use among the ever-increasing A/PI populations in California. Despite the success image of A/PIs as a "model minority," results of this multimethod study provided empirical evidence that Asian/Pacific Islanders in California are not at all immune to AOD use or abuse. For example, although the A/PI populations *as a whole* report relatively low rates of alcohol and related problems, including low treatment admission rates and age-adjusted mortality due to chronic liver diseases and cirrhosis, alcohol still appears to be endemic to all of the A/PI groups studied. As noted earlier, treatment admission rates probably do not reflect the actual number of people who need treatment, but indicate service under-utilization rather than a lower need for services. Also, cigarettes and tobacco products are commonly used, often excessively, by a large number of individuals in the A/PI communities. Other hard drugs such as marijuana, crack cocaine and methamphetamine ("ice") are also prevalent among some of the more established Asian groups, such as the Japanese, and also among the immigrants whose mother countries have a more lenient policy on drug trafficking.

In determining the prevalence of AOD use in the A/PI communities, several methodological and conceptual problems became apparent in the present needs assessment. First, the categories for A/PI, particularly Southeast Asians, are often excluded or lumped together under "Other" or all-inclusive "Asians" in many of the archived data sets examined (e.g., health and mortality, school dropout rates). The assumption here is that because the number of Asians represented is too small to consider separately, AOD use or abuse patterns for any one Asian group can be generalized to all others. The tendency to lump the ever-growing diverse A/PI groups into a single category ignores significant differences among various A/PI populations, thus making it impossible to accurately estimate AOD use prevalence.

Second, although general difficulties associated with prevalence estimation have been noted (Rouse, Kozel, & Richards, 1985), AOD use prevalence among A/PIs presents additional problems. For instance, it is unknown to what extent culturally anchored response biases (e.g., social desirability) enter into measurement errors with A/PI responses. The use of some substances, especially alcohol, seems culturally sanctioned to the extent that males are encouraged or expected to consume alcohol as a sign of "masculinity." In many A/PI cultures, alcohol drinking is well accepted and is part and parcel of Asian cultural events in the communities. Therefore, in the present Community Telephone Survey, some subgroup differences were found in that approximately 90% of the Korean community residents perceived the problem of AOD use as serious or moderately serious, whereas other Asian groups estimated the alcohol problem as less serious (60%-75%). Such ethnic differences in the definition of "substance abuse" as a potential source of measurement errors needs to be investigated in future research.

A third constraint in AOD prevalence estimation is sampling methodology. Although the use of ethnic surnames is an acceptable means of sampling, the true random sampling with A/PI populations is desirable but difficult to attain mainly because of geographical dispersion and unknown cultural factors. An innovative method for selecting representative A/PI populations is clearly needed because those "rare and elusive" (Sudman, Sirken, & Cowan, 1988) individuals considered at risk for substance abuse are often neglected in ethnic minority research. Although the Client Focus Group Study attempted to recruit many of the high-risk individuals in the local Asian communities (e.g., recent immigrants with limited English proficiency, the homeless, and gang members), it was often difficult to identify and locate many of them. Given that AOD use and gang violence are highly interrelated activities among African-American and Hispanic-American communities, it is important to obtain information on AOD use among Asian/Pacific youth gangs. Unfortunately, there is virtually no systematic research for A/PI communities, except for some ethnographic interviews with a few Asian gang members (e.g., Chin, 1990; Vigil & Yun, 1990), which seem to indicate that Asian gang members are involved in drug trafficking but they are not drug users.

Fourth, the paucity of empirical research with the A/PI populations hampers the progress of work on AOD prevelance estimation. For example, there is a great need for the work on Asian substance abuse to converge with previous research that has identified important predictors of AOD use. Cultural variables can be examined in terms of how their effects on substance use and abuse are mediated by certain common sociopsychological processes (e.g., loss of control, peer cluster relationships, lack of personal and social skills). In view of current research emphases in Asian American health and mental health, the most promising areas of convergence would be in research on family cohesion, peer relationships, and stressful life events in terms of cultural adjustment (see Zane & Sasao, in press, for further discussion).

Most of all, a strong need for initiating and maintaining a continuous statewide needs assessment of substance abuse among Asian/Pacific Islander Americans is self-evident.

Summary

This chapter has reviewed the empirical literature and research on the epidemiology of AOD use and abuse among the A/PI Americans. Despite the increasing diversity and numbers of A/PIs in the United States, there is a paucity of studies that investigated culturally specific issues related to AOD use. Some of the methodologial and conceptual issues have been pointed out in the chapter.

Findings of the 1990 California Statewide Asian Drug Needs Assessment were briefly described, noting methodogical and conceptual difficulties in accurately estimating AOD prevalence among A/PI communities.

In the midst of increasing costs for providing needed prevention and treatment services, a greater understanding and accurate portrayal of AOD use and abuse in the A/PI populations is important to guide the practical decisions for resource allocation, program planning, and other purposes. Creativity in designing and implementing culturally appropriate AOD research should facilitate accountability for prevention and treatment services .

Notes

1. On July 1, 1991, CAL-DADS was replaced by the California Alcohol & Drug Data System (CALADDS) in order to incorporate alcohol information.

2. Another component of the present needs assessment, Drug Services Survey (DSS), will not be discussed in the chapter because the primary purpose of the DSS was to assess the availability and current utilization of drug services, as well as the nature of administrative or psychosocial barriers to clients of Asian/Pacific Islander origin.

3. The community forums in three geographical regions were held for the following ethnic communities: Chinese, Japanese, Korean, Filipino, Vietnamese, Samoan, Cambodian (Los Angeles and San Diego only), Laotian and Hmong (San Diego only), and Thai (Los Angeles only). The client focus groups included the following ethnic communities: Chinese (Los Angeles and San Francisco only), Japanese, Korean, Filipino, Vietnamese (San Francisco and San Diego only), Cambodian (San Diego only), Laotian (San Diego only), and Samoan (Los Angeles and San Diego only).

4. Although other AOD use indicators (e.g., non-fatal emergency data) were collected, they were generally unusable due to either small numbers represented or unspecified ethnicity.

References

Adlaf, E. M., Smart, R. G., & Tan, S. H. (1989). Ethnicity and drug use: A critical look. *International Journal of the Addictions, 24*(1), 1-18.
Aoki, B., Ngin, C. P., Mo, B., & Ja, D. (1989). AIDS Prevention models in Asian American communities. In V. M. Mays, G. W. Albee, & S. F. Schneider (Eds.), *Primary prevention of AIDS* (pp. 290-308). London: Sage.
Asian, Inc. (1978). *Assessment of alcohol abuse service needs among Asian Americans in San Francisco.* Unpublished manuscript.

Asian Week, Inc. (1991). *Asians in America: 1990 census.* San Francisco: Author.

Austin, G. A., Prendergast, M. L., & Lee, H. (1989). Substance abuse among Asian American youth. *Prevention Research Update, 5,* 1-28.

Brewer, J., & Hunter, A. (1989). *Multimethod research: A synthesis of styles.* Newbury Park, CA: Sage.

Cahalan, D., & Cisin, I. H. (1976). Drinking behavior and drinking problems in the United States. In G. Kissin & H. Begleiter (Eds.), *Social aspects of alcoholism* (pp. 77-115). New York: Plenum.

Campbell, D. T., & Fiske, D. W. (1959). Covergent and discriminant validation by the multitrail-multimethod matrix. *Psychological Bulletin, 56,* 81-105.

Chin, K.-L. (1990). Chinese gangs and extortion. In C. R. Huff (Ed.), *Gangs in America* (pp. 129-145). Newbury Park, CA: Sage.

Denzin, N. (1970). *The research act.* Chicago: Aldine.

Johnson, B., & Nishi, S. (1976). Myths and realities of drug use by minorities. In P. Iiyama, S. Nishi, & B. Johnson (Eds.),*Drug use and abuse among U.S. minorities.* New York: Praeger.

Johnson, R. C., Nagoshi, G. T., Ahern, F. M., Wilson, J. R., & Yuen, S.H.L. (1987). Cultural factors as explanations for ethnic group differences in alcohol use in Hawaii. *Journal of Psychoactive Drugs, 19*(1), 67-75.

Kitano, H. H. L., & Chi, I. (1985). Asian Americans and alcohol: The Chinese, Japanese, Koreans, and Filipinos in Los Angeles. In D. Spiegler, D. Tate, S. Aitken, & C. Christian (Eds.), *Alcohol use among U.S. ethnic minorities* (pp. 373-382). Rockville, MD: NIAAA.

Kitano, H. H. L., & Daniels, R. (1988). *Asian Americans: Emerging minorities.* Englewood Cliffs, NJ: Prentice-Hall.

Kitano, H. H. L., Lubben, J. E., & Chi, I. (1988). Predicting Japanese American drinking behavior. *International Journal of the Addictions, 23*(4), 417-428.

Klatsky, A. L., Friedman, G., Siegelaub, A. B., & Gerard, M. J. (1977). Alcohol consumption among white, black, or Oriental men and women. *American Journal of Epidemiology, 105,* 311-323.

Kramer, M., & Zane, N. (1984). Projected needs for mental health services. In S. Sue & T. Moore (Eds.), *The pluralistic society: A community mental health perspective* (pp. 47-76). New York: Human Sciences Press.

Lubben, J. E., Chi, I., & Kitano, H. H. L. (1989). The relative influence of selected social factors on Korean drinking behavior in Los Angeles. *Advances in Alcohol and Substance Abuse, 8*(1), 1-17.

Maddahian, E., Newcomb, M. D., & Bentler, P. M. (1985). Single and multiple patterns of adolescent substance use: Longitudinal comparisons of four ethnic groups. *Journal of Drug Education, 15*(4), 311-326.

Maddahian, E., Newcomb, M. D., & Bentler, P. M. (1986). Adolescents' substance use: Impact of ethnicity, income, and availability. *Advances in Alcohol and Substance Abuse, 5*(3), 63-78.

McCarthy, W. J., Newcomb, M. D., Maddahian, E., & Skager, R. (1986). Smokeless tobacco use among adolescents: Demographic differences, other substance use, and psychological correlates. *Journal of Drug Education, 16*(4), 383-402.

McLaughlin, P. G., Raymond, J. S., Murakami, S. R., & Gilbert, D. (1987). Drug use among Asian Americans in Hawaii. *Journal of Psychoactive Drugs, 19*(1), 85-94.

Murakami, S. R. (1989). An epidemiological survey of alcohol, drug, and mental health problems in Hawaii: A comparison of four ethnic groups. In D. Spiegler, D. Tate, S. Aitken, & C. Christian (Eds.), *Alcohol use among U.S. ethnic minorities* (Research Monograph No. 18) (pp. 343-353). Washington, DC: Government Printing Office.

Murase, K. (1977). Delivery of social services to Asian Americans.In National Association of Social Workers (Ed.), *The encyclopedia of social work.* New York: NASW.

Nakashima, J. (1986). Substance abuse: The dark side of "Nikkei Boulevard." *Rice Paper, 10,* 1-3.

Namkung, P. S. (1976). Asian American drug addiction—the quiet problem. In P. Iiyama, S. M. Nishi, & B. Johnson (Eds.), *Drug use and abuse among U.S. minorities.* New York: Praeger.

National Institute on Drug Abuse (NIDA). (1980). *A strategy for local drug abuse assessment.* Washington, DC: Government Printing Office.

National Institute on Drug Abuse (NIDA). (1990). *National household survey on drug abuse: Population estimates 1988.* Washington, DC: Government Printing Office.

Newcomb, M. D., Maddahian, E., Skager, R., & Bentler, P. M. (1987). Substance abuse and psychosocial risk factors among teenagers: Associations with sex, age, ethnicity, and type of school. *American Journal of Drug and Alcohol Abuse, 13,* 413-433.

Phin, J. G., & Phillips, P. (1978). Drug treatment entry patterns and socioeconomic characteristics of Asian American, Native American, and Puerto Rican clients. In A. J. Schecter (Ed.), *Drug dependence and alcoholism: Vol. 2. Social and behavioral issues.* New York: Plenum.

Riley, W. J., Wagenfeld, M. O., & Sonnard, S. (1981). Triangulated investigating: An approach to the estimation of the extent of heroin use. *International Journal of the Addictions, 16*(1), 97-108.

Robins, L. N. (1985). *Studying drug abuse.* New Brunswick, NJ: Rutgers University Press.

Rouse, B. A., Kozel, N. J., & Richards, L. G. (Eds.). (1985). *Self-report methods of estimating drug abuse: Meeting current challenges to validity* (National Institute on Drug Abuse Research Monograph Series No. 57). Washington, DC: Government Printing Office.

Sasao, T. (1990, March). *Substance abuse among Asian/Pacific Islanders: Current trends and research issues.* Paper presented at the conference sponsored by Asian American Recovery Services, Meeting the Challenge of High-Risk Asian Youth in the 90's, San Francisco.

Sasao, T. (1991a). *California statewide Asian drug abuse needs assessment: A multi-method approach* (final report). Sacramento: California State Department of Alcohol and Drug Programs.

Sasao, T. (1991b). *Perception of substance use in a Southern California Japanese community.* Manuscript submitted for publication.

Sasao, T. (in preparation). *Toward an integrative-collaborative framework of research in ethnic minority communities.*

Siegel, L. (1988). *AIDS and substance abuse.* Binghamton, NY: Haworth.

Skager, R., Fisher, D. G., & Maddahian, E. (1986). *A statewide survey of drug and alcohol use among California students in grades 7, 9, and 11.* Sacramento: Office of the Attorney General, Crime Prevention Center.

Skager, R., Frith, S. L., & Maddahian, E. (1989). *Biennial survey of drug and alcohol use among California students in grades 7, 9, and 11: Winter 1987-1988.* Sacramento: Office of the Attorney General, Crime Prevention Center.

Sudman, S., Sirken, M. G., & Cowan, C. D. (1988). Sampling rare and elusive populations. *Science, 240*, 991-996.

Sue, S., & Morishima, J. K. (1982). *The mental health of Asian Americans*. San Francisco: Jossey-Bass.

Sue, S., Zane, N., & Ito, J. (1979). Alcohol drinking patterns among Asian and Caucasian Americans. *Journal of Cross-Cultural Psychology, 10*(1), 41-56.

Trimble, J. E., Padilla, A., & Bell, C. S. (1987). *Drug abuse among ethnic minorities*. Rockville, MD: National Institute on Drug Abuse.

U.S. General Accounting Office. (1990). *Asian Americans: A status report*. Washington, DC: Author.

Vigil, J. D., & Yun, S. C. (1990). Vietnamese youth gangs in Southern California. In C.R. Huff (Ed.), *Gangs in America* (pp. 146-162). Newbury Park, CA: Sage.

Wong, H. Z. (1985). *Substance use and Chinese American youths: Preliminary findings on an interview survey of 123 youths and implications for services and programs*. Unpublished manuscript, The Richmond Area Multi-Services, Inc., San Francisco.

Yee, B.E.K., & Thu, N. D. (1987). Correlates of drug use and abuse among Indochinese refugees: Mental health implications. *Journal of Psychoactive Drugs, 19*(1), 77-83.

Zane, N., & Sasao, T. (in press). Research on drug abuse among Asian Pacific Americans. In J. E. Trimble, C. S. Bolek, & S. J. Niemcryk (Eds.), *Ethnic and multicultural drug abuse: Perspectives on current research*. New York: Haworth.

2

Understanding Criminal Activity and Use of Alcohol and Cocaine Derivatives by Multi-Ethnic Gang Members

MARIO R. DE LA ROSA
FERNANDO I. SORIANO

Introduction

Throughout the United States there is growing concern over the increased proliferation of gangs, delinquency, and the violence associated with both. In one of the most recent national surveys of gangs, Spergel and colleagues (1990) found gangs to be present throughout the United States in many types of communities—large and small, rural and urban. This survey estimated that there are considerably more than 1,439 gangs and 120,636 gang members represented in the cities surveyed. What this recent survey and other surveys (Needle & Stapleton, 1982) have consistently found is a disproportionate number of ethnic minorities as gang members.

Estimates are that more than two-thirds of gang members are ethnic minorities (Spergel and colleges 1989). Numerically, the majority of gangs are either African-American or Hispanic. According to Spergel and colleages (1990), more than half, or approximately 55%, of gang members are African-American, and another third, or 33%, are Hispanic. While these figures may in fact reflect law enforcement's disproportional focus on and adjudication of ethnic minority youths (Miranda, 1987) and an undercount of Anglo non-Hispanic youths, they nevertheless point to incontrovertible gang problems facing ethnic communities throughout the United States.

As with gangs, there is also a growing concern of the proliferation of potent drugs, like cocaine and crack, and their contribution to violence in many ethnic and nonethnic communities. Investigation into the extent and nature of the drug use problem among minority populations has been the subject of much attention during the past decade (Brunswick, 1988; Booth, Castro, & Anglin, 1990; De La Rosa, Khalsa, & Rouse, 1990). The extant epidemiological data on drug usage suggests that the prevalence of illicit drug use is lower among Hispanic and African-American non-Hispanic individuals compared to Anglo individuals (Kopstein & Roth, 1990; Wallace & Bachman, 1991). The research has also pointed to the important role that individual, familial, cultural, socioeconomic, and other environmental factors, such as living in a densely populated large metropolitan area, have on the drug use behavior of minorities, particularly on young African-American non-Hispanic and Hispanic male adolescents (Amaro, Whitaker, Coffman, & Heeren, 1990; Austin & Gilbert, 1989; Brunswick, Merzel, & Messeri, 1985; Caetano & Mora, 1988; Secretary's Task Force on Black and Minority Health, 1985; Szapocznick & Truss, 1978).

I Research to date has yielded valuable information on the relationship between drug use and crime in minority populations (De La Rosa, Lambert, & Gropper, 1990; Dembo et al., 1990; Glick & Moore, 1990; Hamid, 1990; Spunt, Goldstein, Belluci, & Miller, 1990).| Much of the findings from this research have indicated that the high rate of violent criminal behavior found in inner-city African-American and Hispanic communities is either directly related to alcohol and illicit drug use and the illicit drug distribution networks, or due to drug-related gang activities. This research has found that African-American and Hispanic male and female addicts, but particularly heroin addicts, are more likely than their Anglo counterparts to be involved in drug-related violent episodes. According to Spunt et al. (1990) and others, most of these episodes emanate from drug-dealing activities. Less is known, however, on the criminal violent behavior of African-American and Hispanic juvenile cocaine users who are also involved as sellers in the growing crack trade. However, anecdotal information suggests that an increasing percentage of the violence found in African-American and Hispanic inner-city neighborhoods is being committed by juveniles involved in the crack distribution network ("Hour by hour," 1988; "War against drugs," 1989).

Despite the growing research on delinquency, gangs, drugs, and violence, there continues to be a dearth of descriptive research on the magnitude of the drug problem in Hispanic communities (Gfroerer & De La Rosa, under review). Particularly lacking are studies that focus on exploring the role that familial factors play in the initiation, continuation, and escalation of crack use among Hispanic youths. Also needed is research that explores the interrelationship between cocaine use and dealing with violent criminal behavior among Hispanic and African-American non-Hispanic youths.

Further research is also needed that investigates the relationship between drug dealing and delinquent behavior that is often attributed to gang members of various ethnicities. The study reported in this chapter seeks to address some of the gaps mentioned above by providing descriptive information on the violent and nonviolent criminal activities of a group of Anglo, non-Hispanic African-American, and Hispanic male and female juvenile crack users/dealers. The findings from this research are useful to clinicians, educators, and policymakers who need to gain a better understanding of problem youths who are seriously engaged in drug usage and delinquent behavior. Only with better information can human service professionals and policymakers deal more effectively with this growing population of serious delinquents who account for a significant proportion of gangs.

Specifically, the purpose of this chapter is to report on preliminary data pertaining to the use of cocaine and engagement in criminal activities by a non-probability sample comprised of Hispanic, non-Hispanic African-American, and Anglo Saxon "serious" delinquent adolescents from Florida. "Serious" delinquents here refer to youths between 14 and 17 who have committed a minimum of 10 felonies or 100 misdemeanor crimes over the past 12 months. The data reported in this chapter are part of a larger study examining drug use and delinquency (Inciardi, 1989). The chapter is particularly significant in that it is the first to report comparative data on the use of various forms of cocaine (i.e., cocaine powder, paste, and crack) among Hispanic youths who are significantly engaged in delinquent behavior. The study is descriptive in nature, rather than inferential. As such, it relies on the use of descriptive statistics.

Method

Sample Selection and Procedures

As indicated earlier, the data used for this chapter are a part of a larger and more comprehensive study on drug use and delinquency. The data reported in this chapter included the participation of a total of 391 male and 100 female adolescents, ages 12-17, from Miami-Dade County who were considered "serious delinquents." The researchers who collected the data were familiar with the geographic area and with many problem youths in it. Using this familiarity they were able to identify youths who were previously known to them and who met a set of selection criteria. The criteria required that the juveniles be:

- between the ages of 14 and 17
- "seriously" involved in criminal behavior
- Anglo, Hispanic, or non-Hispanic African-American

"Seriously involved" or "serious delinquents" were defined as youths who indicated having committed either a total of 10 or more felonies or 100 or more misdemeanor crimes over the past 12 months. It should be noted that official arrest records or convictions were not used as selection criteria, and the validity of responses was not checked against these.

Numerical quotas for each ethnic group sample were set so that the proportion represented by each subgroup approximated the proportions of ethnic groups arrested and reported in national reporting systems, such as the Uniform Crime Report.

Procedure

Sample selection began by contacting those adolescents meeting the preceding selection criteria who were previously known to the research team. After rapport was established, the snowball method was used, whereby respondents were used to identify peers who would likewise meet the selection criteria and possibly participate in the study. Those being referred were contacted and invited to participate in the study once they met the selection criteria.

Respondents were paid $10 for their participation. Data from all respondents were collected over an 18-month period (1986-1987), with each interview lasting an average of 45 minutes. Respondents participated on a voluntary basis and on conditions of anonymity. Although the procedure for securing respondents limited the generalizability of results, it successfully restricted the pool of participants interviewed to those who were both currently active in the subcultural knit in the street community and considered at risk.

Instrument

A questionnaire consisting of 24 closed-ended items was administered to those who agreed to participate. The items included in the questionnaire elicited information on their social status, family composition, school performance, criminal activities, and drug usage, in particular their use of cocaine and its various derivatives. The questionnaire took approximately 45 minutes to administer. Many of the interviews were conducted in the street and/or in places where the subjects could be found, such as social clubs, bars, parks, and the like.

Field Location

Miami-Dade County in Florida was chosen as the data collection site by researchers for three main reasons: (a) its general urban characteristics, (b) its particular crime and drug-related characteristics, and (c) the research team's prior experience in the area. Miami is a well suited location to conduct research on serious delinquency because it is a large urban area with many of the social problem characteristics of other large cities. The 1980 Census indicated a population of more than 1.6 million, and ranked it 21st in size among Standard Metropolitan Statistical Areas (SMSA) in the United States. Official crime records indicate Miami has unusually high crime rates. For example, the Uniform Crime Reports indicated 10,289 crimes per 100,000 population. This ranked Miami highest in crime of any SMSA in the country, with almost twice the crime rate of the nation as a whole (U. S. Department of Justice, 1990).

Miami is also known for its heavy involvement with various drugs, in particular cocaine and opiates (McBride & McCoy, 1981). It carries the status of being a major import center for illegal drugs. These social problem characteristics made the area well suited for research on seriously involved adolescent delinquents and drug users.

Regarding ethnicity, the population in Miami is culturally diverse and highly appropriate for research on African-Americans and Anglos, but particularly for research on Hispanics. More than half the population is Hispanic, with 67% being of Cuban descent. Puerto Ricans make up the county's second-largest Hispanic population, followed by Nicaraguans, Colombians, and Mexicans. The "other Hispanic" category (i.e., not Cuban, Mexican, or Puerto Rican) has been the fastest growing in recent years, composed of more than 100,000 people in 1980. Although specific information on the ethnic origin of the 100 Hispanics in the sample was not available, we assume that the sample's proportions of Cubans, Puerto Ricans, Mexican-Americans, and other Hispanic groups are similar to those in Miami.

Data Analysis

The analysis conducted for this paper is based on descriptive statistics because of the objective of the paper—to describe the use of cocaine and criminal involvement among Hispanic, African-American, and Anglo adolescent delinquents. Due to the limited access to the data by the authors, statistical tests were not performed on the differences between the response proportions reported. Hence, what is termed "significant" in the text may not be statistically significant. The primary concern here is to report *trends,* similarities, and differences in responses that have face validity or are readily apparent.

Results

Individual and Family Characteristics

The 491 youths in the total sample consisted of 20% Hispanic (n = 100), 40% African-American (n = 198), and 39% Anglo (n = 193). In the total sample, 100, or 20%, were female. Among females, 51 were Anglo (49%) and 49 were African-American (51%). The ages for the entire sample ranged from 14 to 17 years. The mean age for the sample was 15.6 years, and there were no appreciable differences between cultural or gender groups in their mean ages.

Household Characteristics

Household description of respondents indicates no appreciable differences in the male sample, according to ethnicity, in relation to the
person(s) with whom they lived. On the other hand, the data on the
female sample showed that, compared to males, a higher percentage of
them were living with friends or with someone of the opposite sex. That
is, 54.9% of Anglo females and 61.2% of African-American females
lived with their own families, compared to at least 86.6% of any of the
male ethnic or Anglo groups. Hispanics stood out as having the highest
percentage living with their own family, at 91%. If not with their
families, female groups tended to live with friends or members of the
opposite sex (39.2% and 32.6% Anglo and African-American female
groups, respectively).

Other ethnic differences indicate that, in general, African-American
males and females were more likely to come from families where the
female was the head of the household, and the main source of income
was welfare benefits. At least 62.5% of either African-American gender
group came from households dependent on welfare support, compared
to 29.3%, 8.6%, and 21.4% for Hispanic, Anglo male, and female
subgroups, respectively. Family structure may be a probable reason for
these findings, since at least 72.9% of either African-American gender
group came from single-headed households, while 35.7% was the highest for any of the other ethnic or gender groups. Hispanics tended to
come from larger households, with a 4.5 mean number of household
members, compared to no more than 4.0 for any of the other ethnic or
gender groups.

Finally, African-American males and females were less likely to have
family members who were high school graduates or were employed than
their Anglo and Hispanic counterparts. For example, no more than
37.6% of either African-American gender subgroup lived with family
members who were high school graduates, compared to at least 82.8%
of all non-African-American subgroups.

Educational Characteristics

Analysis of educational achievement status levels indicated that there
were only slight differences between males and females by ethnicity.
Altogether, ninth grade was the average grade completed by the youths
in the study. African-American females had the lowest mean number of

years of school completed (8.7), followed by African-American males
(9.0), Hispanic males (9.1), and Anglo males (9.1) and females (9.1).
At least three out of four members (75%) of each ethnic or gender group
were expelled or suspended from school for drug use. However, at 89%,
African-American and Hispanic males had an even greater proportion
who were expelled or suspended. Though the differences were not great,
school-related data showed all ethnic minority subgroups experienced
getting high on drugs at school at an earlier age compared to Anglo
subgroups. That is, the mean grade at which subgroups got high on
drugs was 6.0 for Hispanic males, 6.3 for African-American males, and
5.9 for African-American females, compared to 6.6 and 6.8 for Anglo
males and females, respectively.

Criminal Activities

Table 2.1 lists the percentage of ethnic and gender subgroups who
participated in any of the various crimes listed within the 12 months
prior to the date of the interview. As would be expected due to the
selection criteria, at least 73.5% of adolescents from all other subgroups, except for Anglo females, indicated participating in major
felonies, such as robbery, assault, burglary, and car theft. Aside from
car thefts, African-American males and females tended to have higher
rates of participation in each of the major felony categories.
At least 95.8% of all delinquents in the study indicated participating
in petty property crimes, such as shoplifting. Gender differences were
evident in participation rates in pickpocketing and prostitution theft.
Regarding these two crimes, females indicated substantial participation, particularly with prostitution theft. Similarly, at least 80% of
females of either ethnicity indicated participation in prostitution itself.
Table 2.1 also shows high involvement rates among all study participants in the illegal drug business. With the exception of Anglo females,
at least 91.8% of all other ethnic and gender subgroups indicated
participating in the drug business. Table 2.1 also shows that all study
respondents participated in at least 45 criminal offenses.
When asked which two crimes brought in the most income, at least
80% of Hispanic males included participation in the drug business and
stolen goods as the top two money-making crimes, compared to 69.1%
for African-American males for these same crimes. For 76.5% of Anglo
females and 83.7% of African-American females, prostitution was

Table 2.1 Involvement in Particular Crime Types in the Past 12 Months (Subtotals and Specifics, Percent "Yes")*

| | Male | | | Female | |
| | Hispanic | Anglo | African-American | Anglo | African-American |
	N = 100	N = 142	N = 149	N = 51	N = 49
Major Felony	74.0%	84.5%	87.9%	52.9%	73.5%
Robbery	47.0%	57.0%	75.2%	31.4%	59.2%
Assault	7.0%	14.8%	22.1%	21.6%	24.5%
Burglary	58.0%	65.5%	69.1%	19.6%	63.3%
Motor Vehicle Theft	52.0%	46.5%	49.0%	17.6%	30.6%
Petty Property Crime	99.0%	95.8%	98.7%	98.0%	98.0%
Shoplifting	98.0%	81.7%	94.6%	96.1%	95.9%
Theft From Vehicle	52.0%	73.9%	57.0%	56.9%	46.9%
Pickpocketing	1.0%	2.1%	5.4%	35.3%	30.6%
Prostitute Theft	1.0%	1.4%	1.3%	68.6%	77.6%
Other Larcenies	.0%	9.9%	1.3%	9.8%	2.0%
Confidence Games	20.0%	16.9%	24.2%	35.3%	40.8%
Forgery (Any)	29.0%	27.5%	20.1%	52.9%	46.9%
Stolen Goods Offense	93.0%	64.1%	91.9%	47.1%	71.4%
Property Destruction	28.0%	23.9%	31.5%	17.6%	24.5%
Other Crimes	.0%	.0%	.7%	2.0%	2.0%
Vice Offenses	14.0%	5.6%	20.8%	82.4%	93.9%
Prostitution	3.0%	1.4%	4.7%	80.4%	93.9%
Procuring	11.0%	4.9%	18.8%	51.0%	63.3%
Drug Business	100.0%	95.1%	99.3%	86.3%	91.8%
45+ Offenses	100.0%	100.0%	100.0%	100.0%	100.0%

*Forgery (Any) includes checks, credit cards, and prescriptions. Stolen Goods includes selling, trading, and buying to resell. Property Destruction includes arson (actually, a major felony), but is almost entirely vandalism. Other Crimes were counted with Petty Property Crime, although they mostly were not (e.g., weapons, smuggling, running numbers).

among the top crimes bringing in the most money, followed by the selling drugs, at 52.9% and 83.7%, respectively. For 51% of the Anglo females, petty theft was among the top money-making activities, compared to 37.3% of Anglo males and 20.4% of African-American females who also considered petty theft among the top revenue sources.

Carrying weapons was common to most participants regardless of ethnicity or gender. More than 80% of male delinquents and more than 77% of all females carried lethal weapons on at least 20 or more crimes they participated in over the past 12 months. Handguns were the weapons of choice for all males, followed by knives. At least 64% of Hispanic or African-American males carried handguns with them when committing crimes, compared to 43% of Anglo males, 31.4% of Anglo females, and 20.4% of African-American females. For females, knives were the most favored weapons, followed by handguns. Even so, no less than 3 out of 5 (60%) of any study participant had carried a handgun over the past 12 months.

Substance Use

The results obtained on the drug use patterns of the serious juvenile delinquents interviewed suggested that cocaine (all forms), followed by marijuana, were the drugs preferred most. In particular, Hispanic male serious delinquents, as indicated in Table 2.2, were much more likely than all others in the sample to prefer using cocaine and marijuana over other drugs. It must also be noted that both Anglo males and females and African-American females preferred to drink alcohol at a much higher rate than Hispanic or African-American males.

The pattern of drugs according to ethnicity and gender also indicated that there were some differences in the pattern of cocaine powder, crack cocaine, and cocaine paste use among those interviewed. Table 2.3 shows that Hispanic males and African-American females were more likely to have ever tried cocaine powder, crack cocaine, and cocaine paste at an earlier age, compared to Anglo males and females and African-American males. Cocaine powder was found to be a very popular cocaine derivative among most respondents, but particularly for Hispanic and African-American males. Table 2.3 shows that 100% of Hispanic and African-American males had ever tried cocaine powder and at least 98.7% were at one time regular users of it.

Although the vast majority of adolescents in this study had ever tried crack cocaine and most had at one time been regular users of it, Table 2.3 shows that slightly more Hispanics had higher rates of use, compared to other subgroups. Also, more Hispanic males had tried crack cocaine for a longer period of time, compared to other ethnic groups. Sixty percent of all Hispanic males had first tried crack more than 2 years ago. Hispanic males were followed by African-American females at 51.1%, 47.9% of African-American males, and 30.5% of Anglo males who had first tried crack at least 2 years ago.

In general, cocaine powder and crack were the two most popular forms of cocaine substances with most participants; however, Hispanic

Table 2.2 Drug Preferences

	Male			Female	
	Hispanic	Anglo	African-American	Anglo	African-American
	N = 100	N = 142	N = 149	N = 51	N = 49
Alcohol Type Preferred					
Beer	48.0%	76.1%	69.8%	17.6%	24.5%
Wine, Wine + Beer	30.0%	5.6%	11.4%	27.5%	28.6%
Liquor, Liquor + Other	10.0%	9.2%	6.7%	39.2%	32.7%
None: Don't Like	11.0%	9.2%	11.4%	13.7%	14.3%
Missing Data	1.0%	.0%	.7%`	2.0%	.0%
Named as One of Two Most Preferred Drugs (Percent Yes)					
Cocaine (Any)	100.0%	80.3%	98.0%	94.1%	85.7%
Marijuana	97.0%	75.4%	85.2%	51.0%	73.5%
Alcohol	3.0%	38.7%	8.7%	33.3%	30.6%
Heroin	.0%	1.4%	7.4%	15.7%	8.2%
Rₓ Depressants	.0%	2.1%	.7%	3.9%	.0%
Speed	.0%	.7%	.0%	2.0%	.0%
Inhalant/Hallucinogen	.0%	.7%	.0%	.0%	.0%
The Two Drugs Most Preferred					
Cocaine and Marijuana	97.0%	56.3%	83.2%	47.1%	59.2%
Cocaine and Alcohol	3.0%	21.8%	6.7%	31.4%	20.4%
Alcohol and Marijuana	.0%	16.9%	2.0%	.0%	12.2%
Cocaine and Heroin	.0%	1.4%	7.4%	13.7%	6.1%
Other	.0%	3.5%	.7%	7.8%	2.0%

males tended to use cocaine powder and crack more frequently, compared to the other ethnic or gender groups. Sixty-two percent of Hispanic males were either daily or regular (3+ times per week) users of cocaine powder, compared to 56.4% of African-American males, 47.1% of Anglo females, 46.9% of African-American females, and 31.4% of Anglo males. Regarding crack, 82% of Hispanic males were daily or regular users, compared to 74.5% of Anglo females, 69% of African-American males and females, and 53.6% of Anglo males.

Table 2.3 Drug Use History: Cocaine (Mean Ages and Percentages Involved)*

	Male			Female	
	Hispanic	*Anglo*	*African-American*	*Anglo*	*African-American*
	N = 100	*N = 142*	*N = 149*	*N = 51*	*N = 49*
Cocaine Powder					
First Tried	12.3	13.3	12.4	13.3	12.1
% Ever	100.0%	98.6%	100.0%	100.0%	95.9%
Regular Use	13.2	13.8	13.1	13.7	12.9
% Ever	99.0%	88.7%	98.7%	98.0%	91.8%
Crack Cocaine					
First Tried	13.8	14.3	14.0	14.5	13.8
% Ever	98.0%	92.3%	96.1%	96.1%	91.8%
Regular Use	14.5	14.6	14.4	14.9	14.2
% Ever	92.0%	76.8%	87.9%	88.2%	87.8%
Coca Paste					
First Tried	14.9	15.3	15.2	15.6	14.8
% Ever	13.0%	14.1%	15.4%	9.8%	18.4%
Regular Use	15.0	16.0	15.5	N/A	16.0
% Ever	1.0%	2.1%	1.3%	0.0%	2.0%
Estimated Number of Years Since First Tried Crack**	N = 98	N = 131	N = 144	N = 49	N = 45
Less Than 1	7.1%	17.6%	4.9%	16.3%	15.6%
1 or 2	32.7%	51.9%	47.2%	55.1%	33.3%
2 or 3	37.8%	12.2%	39.6%	18.4%	22.2%
3 or 4	22.4%	18.3%	8.3%	10.2%	28.9%

* "Regular" means three or more times per week.
** Estimate is based on ages: age at interview minus age when first tried crack. Less than one means the two ages were the same. Using ranges for the other categories allows for variations according to when during a year, relative to one's birthday, the use first occurred (i.e., the logical extreme is from the day of a birthday to the day before a birthday).

Discussion

The purpose of the present study was to provide descriptive data on the use of substances and criminal patterns of serious delinquents who had committed a minimum of 10 felonies or 100 misdemeanors over the past 12 months from the time of the interview. Because of the participation of youths from Hispanic, African-American, and Anglo Saxon cultural groups, cross-cultural trends were highlighted. This study also included subgroups of Anglo and African-American females, which allowed for gender comparisons. The results presented were relevant to those concerned about gangs and violent youths, since those in the study demonstrated a commitment to crime and drug use—two characteristics tied to many youth gangs.

The results of the present study revealed differences in the family and household characteristics of delinquents, depending on their ethnic background and gender. Hispanics were found to be more likely to live with family and less likely to come from a female-headed household, compared to other ethnic or gender groups in the study. Hispanics also tended to come from larger families. Compared to males, more females tended to live with friends, including those of the opposite sex.

Regarding criminal involvement, the results showed that the majority of serious delinquent youths participated in major felonies, but particularly in petty crimes, such as shoplifting. Except for mainly Hispanics, the felonies of choice for most youths were largely robberies and burglaries. Car thefts were far more popular with Hispanics than with others. Females were more likely to participate in prostitution-related crimes, such as prostitution theft and prostitution itself. However, the vast majority of youths (more than 86%) participated in the drug business.

Data on drug use showed that for most youths, cocaine powder and crack were used on a regular basis by at least 3 out of 4 youths in the study (76.8%). Although about 1 out of 5 youths had ever tried coca paste, less than 2% used it regularly. Hispanic males stood out as having higher rates of use and preferences for cocaine powder and crack. Also disturbing was the longer time period since first trying crack (60% having tried crack more than 2 years before the time of the interview) compared to other ethnic or gender groups. This suggested Hispanics had a more lengthy experience with crack.

What makes these findings on Hispanic male drug use patterns so disturbing is the substantially lower percentage of Hispanics who indicated they had ever sought drug or alcohol abuse treatment. Only 7% of Hispanic male youths indicated having participated in substance abuse treatment, compared to 32% of Anglo males and a combined 12% for females and African-American male youths.

The level of participation in serious felony crimes, such as robberies, and the use of lethal weapons, such as handguns, by the youths in this study are particularly troublesome. These characteristics, coupled with the prominent use of hard drugs, increase the likelihood of participating in violence leading to serious injuries or homicides (De La Rosa, Lambert, & Gropper, 1990).

What this study failed to ascertain was the peer and social patterns of these youths. For example, we do not know the proportion of youths who participate in youth gangs or cliques. It may be that many of the youths in this study are gang members; however, Moore (Glick & Moore, 1990) warns against assuming a causal relationship between gangs and violence. Instead, Moore suggests that violence can be more appropriately tied to specific activities, such as drug sales. While acknowledging no causal relationship, many contemporary gangs develop close ties either with drug trafficking or with drug use.

While provocative and illuminating, the results of this study are not meant to be directly generalizable to either gang members or to even all serious delinquent youths of the same age range as those in the present study. The sample selection method does no allow for definite generalizability of the results. Further research, utilizing a more random selection method, is needed for comparison with the results of this study. In general, more cross-cultural research is needed that allows for more specific profiles of serious delinquent youths by cultural backgrounds. Research on Hispanic youths is seriously lacking. The findings in this study on Hispanics reflect unique criminal and substance use patterns, which point to the importance of further studying Hispanic populations. This study also suggests that future research should continue to collect data on female delinquents, since their patterns are likewise unique and since we have even less information on them. It is unfortunate that Hispanic females were not included in this study.

In summary, the results of this study point both to the formidable problems surrounding serious delinquent youths and to the need to develop effective prevention and intervention efforts. Researchers have found that a significant proportion of major crimes are committed by a relatively small number of individuals, such as the serious delinquents in the present study. Effective and culturally sensitive intervention efforts are sorely needed to bring to a halt the soaring levels of violence in the United States. In particular, as these results showed, there is a need to better understand the relationship between culture and detrimental behavior, such as crime, drugs, and violence. In doing so, there is a critical need for developing a better understanding of what we mean by intervention efforts that are "culturally sensitive" (Soriano, 1992).

It is clear that the heterogeneity in the U.S. population necessitates socially and culturally specific prevention and intervention programmatic efforts that are tailored to meet the needs of particular ethnic and geographic communities. This does not negate the importance of better understanding the needs common to various heterogeneous groups. However, the historical trend to push for the development of singular intervention and prevention programs that are appropriate for all cultures and communities may now be inadequate. Only culturally and socially sensitive research can lead to the information necessary for developing truly effective prevention and intervention programs that are appropriate for serious delinquent youths, such as those who were the focus in this study.

References

Amaro, H., Whitaker, R., Coffman, M. S., & Heeren, T. (1990). Acculturation and marijuana and cocaine use: Findings from HHANES 1982-84. *Journal of Public Health* (Supp.), 54-60.

Austin, G. A., & Gilbert, M. J. (1989). Substance abuse among Latino youths. *Prevention Research Update, 3*, 1-26.

Booth, M. W., Castro, F. G., & Anglin, D. M. (1990). In R. Glick & J. Moore (Eds.), *Drugs in Hispanic communities* (pp. 21-44). New Brunswick, NJ: Rutgers University Press.

Brunswick, A. F. (1988). Drug use and affective distress: A longitudinal study of urban youths. *Advances in Adolescent Mental Health, 3*, 101-125.

Brunswick, A. F., Merzel, C., & Messeri, P. (1985). Drug use initiation among urban black youths: A seven year follow-up of developmental and secular influences. *Youth and Society, 17*, 189-216.

Caetano, R., & Mora, M. E. (1988). Acculturation and drinking among people of Mexican descent in Mexico and the United States. *Journal of Studies on Alcohol, 49*, 462-471.

De La Rosa, M. R., Khalsa, J. H., & Rouse, B. A. (1990). Hispanics and illicit drug use: A review of recent findings. *International Journal of the Addictions, 25*, 665-691.

De La Rosa, M. R., Lambert, E., & Gropper, G. (1990). *Drugs and violence: Causes, correlates, and consequences* (NIDA Research Monograph No. 103. DHHS Pub. No. (ADM) 91-1721). Washington, DC: Government Printing Office.

Dembo, R., Williams, L., La Voie, L., Getreu, A., Berry, E., Genung, L., Schmeidler, J., Widh, E. D., & Kern, J. (1990). A longitudinal study of the relationship among alcohol use, marijuana/hashish use, cocaine use and cohort of high risk youths. *International Journal of the Addictions, 25*, 1333-1374.

Gfroerer, J., & De La Rosa, M. R. *Protective and risk factors associated with drug use among Hispanic youth.* Manuscript submitted for publication.

Glick, R., & Moore, J. (1990). Drugs in Hispanic communities. New Brunswick, NJ: Rutgers University Press.

Hamid, A. (1990). The political economy of crack-related violence. *Journal of Contemporary Drug Problems, 17,* 31-78.

Hour by hour: Crack, the junkies, the jailers, the pimps, the tiniest addicts. (1988, November 28). *Newsweek,* pp. 64-65.

Inciardi, J. (1989). *Preliminary notes on the problem of "crack" use among serious juvenile delinquents.* Submitted to the National Institute on Drug Abuse, Rockville, MD.

Kopstein, A. N., & Roth, P. (1990). *Drug use among race/ethnic minorities.* Unpublished report, National Institute on Drug Abuse.

McBride, D. C., & McCoy, C. B. (1981). Crime and drug-using behavior. *Criminology, 19,* 281-302.

Miranda, A. (1987). *Gringo justice.* South Bend, IN: University of Notre Dame Press.

Needle, J. A., & Stapleton, W. V. (1982). *Police handling of youth gangs.* Washington, DC: National Juvenile Justice Assessment Center.

Secretary's Task Force on Black and Minority Health, U.S. Department of Health and Human Services. (1985). *Vol. I: Summary.* Washington, DC: Government Printing Office.

Soriano, F. I. (1992). Cultural sensitivity and gang interventions. In A. Goldstein & R. Huff (Eds.), *The gang intervention handbook.* Champaign, IL.

Spergel, I. A., Curry, D., Chance, R., Kane, C., Ross, R., Lexander, A., Simmons, E., & Oh, S. (1990). *Youth gangs: Problem and response; state 1: Assessment.* Washington, DC: Office of Juvenile Justice and Delinquency Prevention.

Spergel, I. A., Ross, R. E., Curry, G. D., & Chance, R. (1989). *Survey of youth gang problems and programs in 45 cities and 6 states.* Washington, DC: Office of Juvenile Justice and Delinquency Prevention.

Spunt, B. J., Goldstein, P. J., Belluci, P. A., & Miller, T. (1990). *Journal of Psychoactive Drugs, 22,* 293-303.

Szapocznick, J., & Truss, C. (1978) Intergenerational sources of conflict in Cuban mothers. In M. Montiel (Ed.), *Hispanic families.* Washington, DC: COSSMHO.

U. S. Department of Justice. (1990). *Uniform crime reports: 1990.* Washington, DC: Government Printing Office.

Wallace, J. M., & Bachman, J. G. (1991). Explaining racial/ethnic differences in adolescent drug use: The impact of background and lifestyle. *Social Problems, 38,* 333-357.

War Against Drugs: Scorn on besieged streets. (1989, September 8). *The New York Times,* p. 4.

PART II

Legal and Policy Issues

3

The Public Health Model and Violence Prevention

PAUL D. JUAREZ

Introduction

Violence is deeply ingrained in the history and social fabric of our nation (Novello, 1991). While few people consider themselves at risk of being a victim of violence, at least 2.2 million people are intentionally injured by someone else each year (U.S. Public Health Service, 1990). As with AIDS, many people in our society have disassociated themselves from being at risk for violence victimization, preferring to believe it is only "those people" who are. While there is growing evidence that certain behaviors and conditions increase the risk for being a victim of violence, the numbers of people affected are so overwhelming that few people are left unscathed by its impact. There is an emerging consensus that something different needs to be done to thwart the explosive growth in violence we are witnessing in our society.

Historically, violence control efforts have been implemented by law enforcement and the criminal justice and social service systems. Yet, efforts to "get tough" on gangs, guns, and drugs by pouring large amounts of money into legal interventions have been largely ineffective. The public health model offers an alternative to traditional criminological and sociological paradigms for conceptualizing the determinants of violence, measuring its impact, and reducing its effect. One of the major shifts brought about by the public health approach is its position that violence is preventable (Rosenberg & Mercy, 1991).

We are at a crossroads in the debate about how to control the epidemic of violence in our society. This debate will shape an emerging social policy on how we as a society address violence. Assumptions about the causes of violence will affect the types of solutions that are put forward and the direction of future funding. It is of critical importance, therefore, that policy decisions are grounded in theory and empirical evidence and not left to sensation-seeking agendas, which sell papers and get officials elected.

This chapter is presented in four sections. It begins with a presentation of the public health model (i.e., agent-host-environment) as an alternative approach to conceptualizing violence prevention and control. A brief overview of the social context of violence in our society is given in the second section, in which the socio-historical role of guns, gangs, and drugs is described. In the last two sections, policy and program implications of a public health approach for violence prevention policy are discussed.

The Public Health Model

Public health officials have recently identified intentional injury as one of the leading threats to the nation's health in terms of morbidity, mortality, disability, and uncontrollable health care expenditures (USDHHS, 1986). Intentional injury describes a range of acts of physical violence, including homicide, suicide, assault, domestic violence, child abuse, elder abuse, gang violence, sexual violence, and hate crimes. Yet all share several common characteristics, including intent, an interpersonal nature, and an outcome that includes physical injury and/or emotional trauma. Homicides alone account for more than 20,000 deaths annually (Rosenberg & Mercy, 1991); and it has been estimated that for every homicide there are approximately 100 nonfatal intentional injuries (U.S. Dept. of Justice, 1988).

The public health model suggests that injury, like infectious disease, can be conceptualized as an interaction between agent, host, and environment (Haddon, 1980). It also suggests that violence is preventable (National Committee for Injury Prevention and Control, 1989). By applying epidemiologic measures to intentional injury, the public health approach offers a methodology for examining conditions that lead to increased risk of intentional injury, for the purpose of developing effective and efficient prevention and intervention efforts.

The Agent

From a public health perspective the agent is the mechanism of injury that results in tissue damage and/or functional impairment. Weapons such as guns and knives are the instruments used in the vast majority of homicides. Firearms have been identified as the mechanism of injury in 50% to 70% of homicides (UCLA & Centers for Disease Control, 1985). Cutting, piercing, and blunt instruments make up most of the remainder.

The Host

The victim of the injury is analogous to the host. Young African-American and Latino males are at a disproportionately high risk of being victims of intentional injuries. African-American and Latino males are approximately 6 times and 3 times more likely to be victims of homicide than white males, respectively (Centers for Disease Control, 1986). Others at increased risk of violence victimization include women, children, the elderly; persons with mental, physical, and developmental disabilities; and sexual and religious minorities. A historical review of the history of violence and oppression in our society suggests they are closely linked.

The Environment

The violence epidemic has been found to be highest among those who live under the most adverse socioeconomic conditions and in communities in which traditional institutions, such as family, church, and schools, are either ineffective or nonexistent. Adverse socioeconomic conditions that have been identified include limited social, recreational, educational, and employment opportunities; high levels of poverty, crime, violence, unemployment, unplanned pregnancy, single-female-headed households, and household size; extant poverty, poor housing conditions, gangs, unemployability of young males, fear, hopelessness, and racism. Low self-esteem and limited connections to the community, also referred to as limited social support systems, have been identified as common characteristics among those at greatest risk for violence (Rosenberg & Mercy, 1991).

Social-Historical Context of Violence

Violence is not merely the outcome of physical aggression that occurs between two or more individuals. Rather, it is a reflection of broad social, economic, and political conditions, which together create an environment that tolerates and even promotes its use. To understand violence, we need to look at it not just as the number of homicides, rapes, or cases of child abuse, elder abuse or domestic violence reported, but also as a common set of conditions that legitimize the use of violence as an acceptable means for fulfilling one's needs and/or wants, in addition to those conditions that perpetuate victimization.

Popular myths about gangs, guns, and drugs severely distort the truth about the nature of violence. It is important that we discern fact from fiction because misguided violence-prevention policies may actually cause more harm than good. Recognition of the socio-historical roles of gangs, guns, and drugs in our society is needed to remind us that efforts to fight violence with greater levels of oppression and force are doomed to failure.

Guns

Firearms are the leading cause of intentional injury mortality and the eighth leading cause of overall death in the United States. Between 1933 and 1982 almost one million persons in this country lost their lives to firearm injuries (Wintenmute, 1987). The total cost of firearm injuries that occurred in 1985 was projected at $370,706 *each* in lost productivity and more than $14.4 billion in lifetime costs (Rice & MacKenzie, 1989).

Guns are not a new problem facing our society. They have long played a pivotal role in our history, as witnessed by the importance given to firearms in Amendment II of the Constitution of the United States, the so-called "right of the people to keep and bear arms." The historical importance of guns in this country is also reflected through our Colonial history, American folklore frontiersmen, outlaws, and modern-day vigilante heroes.

Silberman (1978) called guns "the great equalizer" in our society, suggesting that in the face of so much inequality, particularly for urban ethnic minorities, guns play an important social function. Firearms fulfill individual needs for power, protection, safety, status, and "coming of age" that are no longer being met by traditional social institutions.

Current efforts to control the availability of and/or access to guns that ignore the individual and social needs that firearms fulfill deny their socio-historical importance. Greater attention must be given by public health officials to the role of environmental factors in supporting both violent and nonviolent behavior.

Gangs

Gangs frequently have been identified as the agent of violence. The Los Angeles Police Department reported that as of December 6, 1991, gang membership in the City of Los Angeles totalled 54,956 (Los Angeles Police Department, 1991). The Los Angeles Sheriff's Department estimates that there are more than 100,000 gang members in Los Angeles County (Community Youth Gang Services, 1991). While this figure is now widely quoted, few have questioned how the estimate was derived or what it actually means. It therefore is useful to put it in perspective.

An estimate of 100,000 gang members represents roughly 3% of the total combined African-American and Latino populations of Los Angeles County; 7%—one in 15—of all African-American and Latino males, and 36%—one in three—of all African-American and Latino males, ages 15 to 24, who reside in the County of Los Angeles. And 100,000 is also roughly equivalent to the entire African-American male population between the ages of 13 and 24 that resides in Los Angeles County (U.S. Bureau of Census, 1983). While arguably whites and Asians account for approximately 5% of gang membership in Los Angeles County (LAPD, 1991), it is President Bush's image of "Willie Horton" and Chief Daryl F. Gates's image of "rotten little [African-American and Latino] cowards" that the term *gangbanger* conjures up.

Even if one is to assume that the estimate of 100,000 gang members is accurate, we still don't know what this statistic means. Critical questions are not yet being asked, such as: "How is gang member defined?" "Are all gang members created equal?" "Are gangs inherently bad?" and "Why are so many youths, particularly in the inner cities, turning toward gangs?" These are the questions that have been largely ignored by the media, law enforcement, public officials, the general public, and social scientists alike. Instead, society has seemingly accepted a description of gangs that presents them as a well-oiled, monolithic, or bi-lithic (i.e., the Bloods and the Crips) military and/or corporate force that occupies our inner cities, produces and exports violence, and presents a threat to legitimate enterprise and the "American way of life."

Historically, research and scholarly work have shown gangs in a very different light than the popular media of today present. Gangs have previously been identified in the literature as providing a number of important functions in the socialization of adolescent males, including loyalty, protection, emotional/social support, economic opportunities, and camaraderie. Efforts to get tough with gangs frequently disregard the considerable body of knowledge that exists about gangs and the reasons why youths join and stay in gangs.

While some historical explanations are rejected, either in part or in whole, as plausible descriptions of current gangs, they provide much needed theoretical frameworks for discussing and examining the etiology, dynamics, and structure of gangs and gang behavior that have been totally absent in efforts to understand the increasing wave of gang violence. Theoretical explanations of gangs, gang behaviors, and the organization of gangs have been previously presented by Miller (1958), Cohen (1955), Cloward and Ohlin (1960), Short and Strodtbeck (1965), Glueck and Glueck (1950), Vigil (1988), and Moore (1988).

Miller (1958) argued that gangs are a reflection of a lower-class subculture unaffected by the conventional values of society. Six different concerns of lower-class culture identified by Miller were trouble, toughness, smartness, excitement, fate, and autonomy. According to Miller, gang membership provides opportunities for fulfillment of lower-class norms that place youth on a collision course with the rest of society.

Cohen (1955) described gangs as a reaction formation mechanism through which working-class youths cope with their humiliation, frustration, anxiety, hostility, and bitterness toward the middle class. He argued that gang members express their hostility through attacks on the norms of the middle class, particularly private property.

Cloward and Ohlin (1960) discussed gang behavior within the context of anomie theory and opportunity systems. They argued that youths who have no legitimate opportunities for success in society turn to structurally illegitimate opportunities. Depending on the immediate milieu, illegitimate behaviors were described in terms of criminal, conflict, or retreatist orientation. According to Cloward and Ohlin the level of organization and stability found within the gang is a reflection of the community in which the gang exists.

Short & Strodtbeck (1965) suggested that gang members hold the goals of the larger society, but that these youth strive for status within their own milieu rather than the context established by the society. They argued that the goals of the gang cross class and subculture divisions, are shaped by the dynamics of obtaining status within their own reference group, and are best understood within the context of group dynamics and process.

Glueck and Glueck (1950) identified family environments and biological variables as etiological factors of delinquent behavior. They argued that youths with certain personality traits are more likely to engage in deviant behavior, particularly those who perceive their parents as rejecting and uninterested in their welfare. From this perspective, gangs can be described as providing an alternative supportive environment, which fulfills the developmental needs of male adolescents.

Vigil (1988) suggested that gangs play a particularly important role during the adolescent passage to manhood in those households that engender cross-sex identification (e.g., female-headed households and transient male adult models) and in those homes in which there are problematic personal and/or family backgrounds.

Moore (1988) argued for the importance of understanding the effects of cultural factors on gang structure and behavior. She found that the activities and behaviors of Chicano gangs: (a) can be seen as a symbolic challenge to the world, (b) are innovative and develop within their own logic, and (c) are consistently responsive to certain types of interventions. She also found substantial variation in the level of violence between gangs, even from one clique to another within the same gang. Nothing in the literature on gangs supports the notion that id-driven male adolescents from low socioeconomic backgrounds are developmentally capable of maintaining the discipline necessary to operate and function within a rigorously structured organizational setting. Instead, the proliferation of gangs routinely has been described as an unstable phenomenon, linked by a common experience of adolescent males to have their basic needs met within the presenting socio-historical context. Prevention efforts need to address the individual developmental needs that the gang fulfills.

Drugs

Drugs also have been identified as one of the primary vectors of violence in this country. The association between drugs and violence is reinforced by sensational images of narco-traffickers, both here and abroad, and by reports of bizarre behaviors of people under the influence of drugs, chiefly PCP. Yet the use of drugs has a long-standing history in this country. While the illicit substance of choice has changed over the years from opium to cocaine, heroin, marijuana and designer drugs, heavy use of alcohol in our society has remained constant.

Even today, despite massive efforts to reduce drugs through supply-side interdiction strategies, the use of drugs goes on at near-record levels. A recent report indicated that 2 in every 100 people in the United States are hard-core cocaine addicts. In a national sample of lifetime use of drugs by high school seniors (Johnston, Bachman, & O'Malley, 1986) found that 10% had used opiates, 17.3% had used cocaine, 26.2% had used amphetamines, 54.2% had used marijuana, and 92.2% had used alcohol on at least one occasion. The social and economic costs of substance abuse in the United States have been estimated at more than $200 billion a year.

The National Household Survey on Drug Abuse (USDHHS, 1989) reported 14.5 million persons in the United States had used an illicit drug within 30 days of the interview. While declines were found in most categories of substance abuse as compared to a 1985 study, the number of persons who used cocaine once a week or more increased by more than 33%. Cocaine use was found to be highest among the unemployed, persons age 18 to 25, and persons who resided in Western states and in large metropolitan areas (USDHHS, 1989). While lifetime prevalence of cocaine use was found to have remained stable for whites and African-Americans, Latinos reportedly experienced a dramatic increase from 7% to 11%.

Alcohol continues to be the most commonly used drug. Two-thirds of the sample indicated that they had used alcohol during the month preceding the interview. Of the 135 million persons who drank alcohol in the previous year, more than one third, or 47 million, indicated that they drank once a week or more often. To date, however, the lion's share of the monies targeted toward prevention has gone to law enforcement efforts to stop the flow of drugs, rather than to address the reasons why people use drugs.

Policy Implications: Framing the Issue

The acceptance of violence and of those factors that are associated with its occurrence is deeply entrenched in and perpetuated by our social institutions. The explosive increase in violence, however, can not be explained simply by the existence of guns, gangs, and drugs; these have been with us throughout our history. Rather, it appears that guns, gangs, and drugs are indicators of other social phenomena, and are not themselves the direct causes of violence. If this is the case, efforts to prevent violence through measures to control guns, gangs, and drugs are not likely to be very effective because they ignore the root causes of violence. In order to understand the causes of violence we need a better understanding of the context and processes through which its socialization occurs.

Violence is a manifestation of disenfranchisement of entire communities and segments of our society. The increased rate of violence parallels the decline of relevance of traditional social institutions as a resource for persons trying to cope with a rapidly changing environment. This is most evident in inner cities where the institutions of family, schools, church, culture, and government have not accommodated the changing needs of communities.

Today youths from poor and underserved backgrounds have few social support systems available to help them overcome the normal developmental tasks and social challenges that face them during adolescence and young adulthood. With both fewer ties to traditional social institutions and a dearth of positive role models in their lives, African-American and Latino youths in the inner city have been forced to cope with the transition from adolescence to adulthood in the streets, where guns, gangs, and drugs fulfill normal individual developmental needs of group identity, power, independence and money, personal safety, self-esteem, and status.

The impact of violence has far outstripped the resources and capabilities of the family, schools, church, and other traditional institutions to cope with the new set of demands that has been placed on them. There has been a severe eroding of the integrity of these institutions as primary institutions for socialization, effective social support systems, and advocates and/or buffers for disenfranchised persons.

Myths and stereotypes about guns, gangs, and drugs have resulted in policies and interventions that not only are misguided but also are potentially harmful by virtue of their further exacerbating racist and oppressive tendencies within our society. We cannot continue to fight violence with greater levels of oppression and force. The time has come for us to address the underlying causes of gangs, guns, drugs, and violence before they overwhelm us.

Violence prevention and intervention strategies cannot ignore the oppressive role that social, political, and economic institutions have played historically in promoting the use of violence. For prevention strategies to be effective in underserved and ethnic minority communities, they must take into account not only the high-risk behaviors of the individual, but also the complex and difficult social conditions that have spawned and now support those behaviors. Environmental interventions that either establish or strengthen the ability of traditional social institutions to meet individual developmental needs for loyalty, protection, emotional/social support, economic and recreational opportunities, and camaraderie are likely to have the greatest impact.

Policy Implications: Programs and Strategies

Social policy efforts can be divided into three broad categories of violence prevention interventions: those that target change in (a) the host, (b) the agent, and (c) the environment.

Described below is a review of broad strategies and programs that either currently exist or have been proposed, their aim, and their theoretical basis. Some of the programs are also described by Wilson-Brewer and Jacklin (1990), in the Introduction of the Background Papers, distributed by the Centers for Disease Control, at the December 10-12, 1990, Forum on Youth Violence in Minority Communities: Setting the Agenda for Prevention.

Targeting Individual Change

Public health strategies that promote violence prevention through individual change are consistent with a traditional educational approach. These include didactic interventions aimed at changing individual knowledge, attitudes, and behaviors associated with violence. Categories of educational interventions designed to prevent violence include conflict resolution education and dispute mediation training, firearm safety courses, and general education interventions. A brief description of some of these is presented below.

Conflict Resolution Education

Conflict resolution skills curricula have been designed to help people develop empathy, impulse control, problem-solving skills, and anger management skills as a way to teach alternative nonviolent behaviors

(Prothrow-Stith, 1987). This approach is based on an individual deficit model. It assumes that certain individuals lack effective interpersonal coping skills. Individuals are taught alternative knowledge, attitudes, and behaviors that will help them resolve conflict with others in a more socially acceptable, less violent manner. This approach typically includes a combination of didactic instruction, role playing, and simulation, and is most frequently implemented in a school setting.

Dispute Mediation Training

Dispute mediation training helps students develop the skills needed to mediate interpersonal conflicts. This approach often includes extensive skills development training in the areas of communication, leadership, problem solving, and assertiveness. In some programs students are trained to mediate disputes on a formal case-by-case basis, while in others they are trained to serve as conflict managers in occurrences of daily living. Dispute resolution programs have been implemented in both school and community settings (Wilson-Brewer & Jacklin, 1987).

Firearm Safety Courses

Firearm safety programs include activities whose aim is to reduce violence by teaching students about the dangers of firearms when they are not properly used and/or stored (Northrop & Hamrick, 1990).

Support Groups

Adolescent peer counseling and support groups also have been used, primarily within school settings, to help adolescents develop and improve their communication, coping, and decision-making skills. They are developed most typically as a forum for shaping attitudes rather than for increasing knowledge. This approach recognizes that adolescents are strongly influenced by their peers and that the influence of peers can be structured to provide a positive force in their lives (Northrop, Jacklin, Cohen, & Wilson-Brewer, 1990).

General Education Strategies

A variety of general education strategies, which also have been implemented, have as an indirect objective the prevention or reduction of violence. Drug and alcohol prevention programs, life skills training, social competence training, parenting education programs, and school improvement programs all have been identified as important components in the reduction of violence. While most of these programs target in-school youths, some have also been developed that target out-of-school and other high-risk youths (Ross & Zigler, 1980).

Targeting the Agent of Violence

Social policy efforts that target the agent of violence include activities to make firearms safer through engineering design, litigation, and legislation. They include banning the import, sales, and distribution of firearms; requiring gun registration and background checks; and holding manufacturers of firearms liable for the safety of their products (Northrop & Hamrick, 1990).

Targeting the Environment

The causes of violence are woven into the broader underlying social conditions that plague inner-city, predominantly minority communities. The context of violence is characterized by the inability of people to meet or to have met their basic needs for adequate food, shelter, health care, education, employment, love, and emotional support. Racism, sexism, and classism promote the conditions of oppression, hopelessness, and despair found in ethnic minority communities, and contribute to the disproportionate toll that violence reaps on African-American, Latino, and Native American populations.

Social policy efforts to prevent violence encompass a broad array of activities. In addition to the promulgation of public laws and regulations, violence prevention will require changes in social systems, community organization, and public awareness. Examples of social policy interventions to prevent violence are presented below.

Community Development

Efforts to change social conditions through community development provide another dimension for violence prevention policy. Developing a consensus and sense of ownership of the problem and the solution, and forming advocacy and service referral networks, are important steps in community development. Interventions based in indigenous community-based institutions and agencies are likely to be sensitive to unique cultural and socio-historical issues, have an already established client base, and have gained the confidence and/or trust of the community.

Interventions to Build Male Self-Esteem

Interventions to build male self-esteem differ from didactic approaches because they require changes in social systems, not just changes of individual knowledge, attitudes, and behaviors. Self-esteem cannot be taught in the same way that conflict resolution skills are taught. Building self-esteem requires the existence of local institutions that promote and reinforce a positive sense of self-worth and development among the youths of the community.

A number of different types of programs have been designed to enhance male self-esteem. Interventions to build self-esteem suggest that if a person feels good about himself or herself, he or she will be less likely to engage in behaviors that are destructive to self or others (Wilson-Brewer & Jacklin, 1990).

Manhood Development/Rites of Passage

The need for alternative community support systems that enhance and support self-esteem has been identified as critical for the health of urban minority youth, particularly African-American males. Manhood development curricula that focus on "total development" have been suggested as one strategy. This approach attempts to affect moral development both by teaching Afro-centric values and principles and by providing positive African-American males.

Likewise "rites of passage" programs have been developed to help young males cope with the developmental tasks and social challenges that confront them during their preteen and teenage years. These programs promote increased responsibility, independence, and rights.

Mentors/Role Models

A related approach for increasing male self-esteem is the employment of mentors and/or role models. Through their involvement as teachers, friends, and counselors, mentors present positive adult male role models to youths by sending dual messages that: (a) there are ethnic minority males who function at high levels within society, and (b) ethnic minority youths are worthy of their time and attention (Northrop, Jacklin, Cohen, & Wilson-Brewer, 1990).

Immersion Strategy

Immersion schools have been proposed as a strategy for increasing self-esteem among young African-American males. This strategy suggests that young African-American males would be better served if separate classrooms, taught by male African-American teachers, were established. Immersion schools integrate the mentoring/role model with cultural awareness/determination and manhood development curricula. This approach has not been universally accepted and faces many challenges from both existing social and educational institutions and laws that prevent segregated public schools.

Community Awareness Interventions

Community awareness interventions include a host of strategies whose purpose is to raise the general level of awareness within a defined community. Mass media strategies are used to target a broad community. They frequently include the use of public service announcements on the audio and visual media, use of editorials, mass mailings, and the print media as avenues for informing the community about not only the scope, context, and outcomes of violence but also specific steps that can be taken to either prevent or stop its occurrence. Use of the mass media generally is designed to raise community consciousness about the issues, shape public opinion, increase knowledge, and change attitudes, but not to directly affect individual behavior.

More selective community awareness activities often target narrow strata within a community. They utilize opportunities of limited access such as geographical proximity or service utilization patterns. Establishing contact through selective access can be used to target groups at elevated risk of violence. Public hospitals, clinics, housing units, and street corners provide access to low-income populations; correctional facilities provide access to males with criminal histories; public social service agencies, domestic violence shelters, and family planning clinics provide access to low-income women; local schools, churches, and grocery stores provide access to the general population of a local neighborhood. Increasing community awareness about violence prevention is a critical first step in changing public policy.

Advocacy

Advocacy entails the mobilization of constituencies. Community-based and provider coalitions provide vehicles for advocating change (Cohen & Lang, 1990). Effective community organization requires establishing a shared perception about the causes of violence and its solutions, community ownership of the problem, and a common will to do something about it.

Public Policy

Changes in public policy toward violence prevention can be affected through the legislative, executive, and judicial branches of government: Laws can be passed, regulations promulgated, and litigation filed. Public policy decisions can have a broad or narrow impact, depending upon whether they are enacted at the local, state, or federal level of jurisdiction. The scope of activities that can be pursued through public policy generally is limited to politically palatable decisions.

Conclusion

Historically, policy efforts to reduce violence have targeted the perpetrator as the cause of violence, especially gangs, guns, and drugs. Alternatively, the public health model suggests violence can be prevented by identifying and targeting interventions toward characteristics of the agent, the host, and the environment that place persons at increased risk of intentional injury.

It is not by chance alone that victims of violence are among the most oppressed in our society; yet current public health interventions to reduce violence have focused primarily on the agent and the host. Greater attention needs to be given to social policy interventions that target change in the environment, including advocacy, community awareness, and community development strategies. Ultimately, the prevention and control of intentional injury rests in our ability to address those conditions and institutions in our society that condone and perpetuate the use of violence.

References

Centers for Disease Control. (1986). *Homicide surveillance: High-risk racial and ethnic groups—blacks and Hispanics, 1970 to 1983.* Atlanta, GA: Author.

Cloward, R. A., & Ohlin, L. E. (1960). *Delinquency and opportunity: A theory of delinquent gangs.* New York: Free Press.

Cohen, A. K. (1955). *Delinquent boys: The culture of the gang.* New York: Free Press.

Cohen, S., & Lang, C. (1990). *Applications of principles of community-based programs.* Background paper prepared for Youth Violence in Minority Communities: A Forum on Setting the Agenda for Prevention. Atlanta, GA.

Community Youth Gang Services. (1991). *Gang education, assessment, and planning system.* Los Angeles: Author.

Glueck, S., & Glueck, E. T. (1950). *Unraveling juvenile delinquency.* New York: Commonwealth Fund.

Haddon, W. (1980). Advances in the epidemiology of injuries as a basis for public policy. *Public Health Reports, 95*(5), 411-421.

Johnston, L. D., Bachman, J. G., & O'Malley, P. (1986). Student drug use in America 1975-1981 (DHHS Publicaton No. ADM 82-1208). Rockville, MD: National Institute on Drug Abuse.

Los Angeles Police Department (LAPD). (1991). *November monthly report, citywide gang crime summary.* Los Angeles: Author.

Miller, W. B. (1958). Lower class culture as a generating milieu of gang delinquency. *Journal of Social Issues, 14,* 5-19.

Miller, W. B. (1965). Violent crimes and city gangs. *Annals of the American Academy of Political and Social Science, 364,* 96-112.

Moore, J. (1988). Variations in violence among Hispanic gangs. In J. F. Kraus, S. B. Sorenson, & P. D. Juarez (Eds.), *Research conference on violence and homicide in Hispanic communities* (pp. 215-230). Los Angeles: UCLA Publication Services.

National Committee for Injury Prevention and Control. (1989). *Injury prevention: Meeting the challenge.* New York: Oxford University Press.

Northrop, D., & Hamrick, K. (1990). *Weapons and minority youth violence.* Background paper prepared for the Forum on Youth Violence in Minority Communities: Setting the Agenda for Prevention. Atlanta, GA.

Northrop, D., Jacklin, B., Cohen, S., & Wilson-Brewer, R. (1990). *Violence prevention strategies targeted towards high-risk minority youths.* Background paper prepared for the Forum on Youth Violence in Minority Communities: Setting the Agenda for Prevention. Atlanta, GA.

Novello, A. C. (1991). Violence is a greater killer of children than disease [Special Section]. *Public Health Reports, 106*(3), 231-233.

Prothrow-Stith, D. (1987). *Violence prevention curriculum for adolescents.* Newton, MA: Education Development Center.

Rice, D. P., & MacKenzie, E. J. (1989). *Cost of injury in the United States.* Washington, DC: U.S. Dept. of Health and Human Services.

Rosenberg, M. L., & Mercy, J. A. (1991). Assaultive violence. In M. L. Rosenberg & M. A. Fenley (Eds.), *Violence in America: A public health approach* (pp. 14-50). New York: Oxford University Press.

Ross, C. H., & Zigler, E. (1980). An agenda for action. In G. Gerbna, C. J. Ross, & E. Zigler (Eds.), *Child abuse: An agenda for action* (pp. 293-304). New York: Oxford University Press.

Short, J. A., Jr., & Strodtbeck, F. L. (1965). *Group process and delinquency.* Chicago: University of Chicago Press.

Silberman, C. E. (1978). *Criminal violence and criminal justice.* New York: Vintage Books.

UCLA & Centers for Disease Control. (1985). *The epidemiology of homicide in the city of Los Angeles, 1979-1979.* Atlanta, GA: U.S. Department of Health and Human Services.

U.S. Department of Commerce, Bureau of the Census. (1983). *1980 census of population.* Washington, DC: Government Printing Office.

U.S. Department of Health and Human Services (USDHHS). (1986). Homicide, suicide, and intentional injuries. *Report of the Secretary's task force on black and minority health, volume V.* Washington, DC: Government Printing Office.

U.S. Department of Health and Human Services. (1989). *The national household survey on drug abuse.* Washington, DC: Government Printing Office.

U.S. Department of Justice, Bureau of Justice Statistics. (1988). *Criminal victimization in the United States, 1986: A national crime victim survey report* (NCJ-111456). Washington, DC: Author.

U.S. Public Health Service. (1990). Violent and abusive behavior. In *Healthy people 2000: Conference edition* (pp. 225-246). Washington, DC: USDHHS.

Vigil, J. D. (1988). Street socialization, locura behavior, and violence among Chicano gang members. In J. F. Kraus, S. B. Sorenson, & P. D. Juarez (Eds.), *Research conference on violence and homicide in Hispanic communities* (pp. 231-241). Los Angeles: UCLA Publication Services.

Wilson-Brewer, R., & Jacklin, B. (1990). *Violence prevention strategies targeted at the general population of minority youth.* Background Paper prepared for the Forum on Youth Violence in Minority Communities: Setting the Agenda for Prevention. Atlanta, GA: Centers for Disease Control.

Wintenmute, G. J. (1987). Firearms as a cause of death in the United States, 1920-1982. *The Journal of Trauma, 27*(5), 532-536.

4

The Impact of Gangs and Drugs in the Community

FRED B. MARTINEZ

Introduction

Today the effect of proliferation of gangs is shared by everyone in the community because this "gang problem," as it is frequently referred to, is based on criminal activity and, in many cases, a criminal enterprise for financial gain.

The community finds it difficult to understand not only the rapidly increasing present-day gang activity but also the origins of this gang activity. For decades warfare has raged among these gang groups, based on territorial disputes, family vendettas, and traditional rivalries that sometimes involved only "colors."

This warfare has evolved into a more sophisticated type, which has become a focal point for these gangs. They now use sophisticated weapons with increased regularity in assaults against each other, which consequently has caused a dramatic increase in assaults and homicides in many of the communities where this problem exists. Probably the best known of these types of assaults is the drive-by shooting, which is a popular mode of operation for the majority of these gangs.

According to the Los Angeles County Sheriff's Department's Operation Safe Streets program, which addresses gang-related homicides, in 1979 there were 276 gang-related homicides recorded for that year; in 1991, 771 gang-related homicides were recorded in Los Angeles County. This constitutes a 280% increase since the LASD began collecting such data. It must be noted that there was a period from 1981 to 1984 where there was no major increase in such homicides, due to the introduction of suppression programs that were directed at this gang problem, and that consequently sent many gangbangers (as gang members are often called) to either jail or prison. Then in 1985, the number of gang-related homicides began to increase again. It is speculated that this increase occurred when many of the gangbangers who had been incarcerated were released, and the gang activity became more intense, due to the many gang rivalries that flourished in the jail and prison settings.

Many communities have reported a dramatic increase in gang-related assaults and deaths. This had been attributed to the ability of gangs to become mobile and relocate to other cities, such as Phoenix, Arizona; Las Vegas, Nevada; Kansas City, Missouri; Lubbock, Texas; Denver, Colorado; and Portland, Oregon.

Today, this gang phenomenon has become popular and "chic," in that it has produced a style of dress, language, and music that has provided an avenue for persons of any ethnic group to identify with this gang style.

The information described in this chapter will address all gang groups as one of a kind, as they impact everyone in the community. We can no longer say, "It's those people's problem," or "It's on that side of town, so why should I worry about it?"

This chapter is based on my report, titled *An Analysis of the Impact of Black Gangs From Los Angeles to the Inland Empire* (Martinez, 1988). I was asked by the Department of the Youth Authority to describe the problem related to the influx of black street gangs into Riverside and San Bernardino counties, in Southern California.

Years ago in many communities, there were gang "rumbles," and each neighborhood had its own group that was its gang, who defended the neighborhood territory, or turf. Today communities are expressing concern at gang activity because there are so many more injuries and deaths. This is especially true when the victims are innocent, and in many cases, these innocent victims just live in the area or happen to be in the wrong place at the wrong time. The gang activity today, as in previous years, still involves turf, territorial disputes, and family vendettas, but with an added factor: the lucrative drug business.

Before continuing, I would like to explain that each gang group has distinct characteristics that distinguish it from the others. For many, those characteristics are traditional in nature, the continuation of generations of a life-style and way of life; and for others it is the glory to "live a style" that is celebrated by the characters in many movies, both today and in the past, which are so popular with these gang members.

Theories of Gang Membership

There are many explanations as to how gangs established themselves. Many of these explanations are well established and are used to train and educate professionals in law enforcement, education, and hospital and treatment settings as well as members of the community, especially parents.

As previously stated, generations of tradition have perpetuated some gang groups where brothers, sisters, fathers, mothers, uncles, aunts, grandfathers, and grandmothers may have been "from the neighborhood." They may have claimed an allegiance to their group to the point of being soldiers or guardians of the "hood." Their activities involved using such weapons as sticks, bats, chains, knives, and in some cases, handguns. Today, the use of semiautomatic handguns and assault rifles by these gangs has added "fuel to the fire."

Present-day gang members hear stories from family members of vendettas and the rivalries that have created heroes and given them the need to be like one of those legends. And, along with that "I want to be like" thinking, they become entrenched in a life-style that grows increasingly difficult to escape.

Many of the gangs that exist today are based only on certain interests or associations. Some groups, identifying with Heavy Metal music and groups, soon took on the traditional activity of fighting with other groups of similar interests, but with traditional methods. These interest-type gangs then soon found themselves taking on traditional, older established gangs, which forced them to become traditional in the sense that they either combined with traditional gangs or took on a traditional existence, but maintaining their name.

There are those gangs who become associated with certain colors, that is, red or blue. In the late 1970s, traditional gangs with common neighborhood ties and associations based on friendships soon took on identifications based on colors to distinguish them from other groups. These groups are not always based on defending their territory or turf, only on the philosophy associated with a "color."

The gangs have developed a language, identifying characteristics, and particular styles of dress that utilize sports team logos and colors, which are use to identify particular gangs. For example, a red Philadelphia Phillies baseball cap with the letter "P" on it would represent a "Piru" Blood set (a set is a subgroup of a larger group). This dress style causes particular concern because there are individuals who are not affiliated with gangs and choose to wear the universally popular sports clothing. A gang member could approach someone wearing a Phillies cap and ask, "Where you from?" meaning, "What gang do you belong to?" If the non-gang member is not convincing enough regarding his non-affiliation, he could find himself in the middle of a confrontation. On the other hand, gang members sometimes do not bother to ask questions, but automatically assume that whoever is wearing the particular clothing is a gang member—which often results in the non-member being assaulted or shot.

This matter of clothing is an important issue for parents and school administrators. In some areas of the city, school have chosen to ban all sports-related clothing on campus as a safety measure. For example, one high school allows no baseball caps except those with the school logo. Parents, too, need to be concerned. Beyond the possibility that they are spending considerable money (these jackets, caps, and such are expensive) to satisfy their children's wishes, only to perhaps jeopardize their safety, they would also do well to consider whether the request for such sports-related clothing is an indication that their sons or daughters are beginning to identify with a gang.

It is important to understand the origins of these gangs. They base their existence on tradition and they are part of a trend that the gangs have cultivated, but more importantly, they are motivated by the desire for personal survival, a response to social and racial prejudices, and the need that youths have to "belong." It is these reasons that support the growing belief that gangs are here to stay. Furthermore, continual denial by many communities only reinforces this belief.

The L.A. Connection

This term commonly refers to the fact that many gangs throughout the country have modeled themselves on the Los Angeles type gangs that have received so much media attention. These gangs have established themselves in communities that were traditionally areas without gang activity.

Pressure to Relocate

Many communities like Los Angeles established special gang suppression units within their law enforcement agencies, with the primary function of identifying the gangs and their members, their criminal activity, and the problems they cause in the community that are associated with their activity. These special units utilized every resource in putting these violators in custody. For this reason, many of these gang members soon learned that they could find safe refuge in other cities, counties, and states, where relatives or friends lived. So, in a community where there were one or two persons who identified with a gang or group from Los Angeles, there would now be additional members to add to their cadre of soldiers, making their presence more obvious to the community. This was thought of by the community as "not a problem," just something associated with that cultural group.

Another reason for the L.A. Connection was that whole families were relocating. Many parents of these gang members/associates, who lived in areas with large numbers of gangs, have left or are leaving communities they have lived in for many years, with the hope of changing the behavior of their children and the influences that negative element has had on them.

In addition, the cost of housing has frequently been more affordable in the outlying areas. These outlying areas are commonly referred to by the gang element as "virgin territories," which soon became prime targets for gang activity. Almost always, the result of these geographic moves is unsuccessful when the children and other family members find old neighbors (and gang members) who are also attending the new school or living in the neighborhood. This perpetuates the "homeboy" attitude in the new neighborhood.

Gangs and Drug Activity

Involvement with narcotics is considered a major factor in the increase of gang activity in communities. The Los Angeles County Sheriff's Department reported more than 100,000 identified gang members associated with more than 900 different gang groups. These figures reflect an increase doubled from 1984 figures. Many of these gang groups are involved in the sale or distribution of narcotics. This increase in the number of gangs and members, with many who are dealers, produced competition for the drug profits in the city; and the competition has driven the price of narcotics to an unprofitable low. Gang members involved in the drug business were quick to realize that a substantial profit could be made by relocating to "virgin territories." In some cases, safe houses were established by those gang members who relocated for the sole purpose of dealing narcotics. The recent trend is for many of these gangs to ally themselves with rival gangs to establish a stronger organized group.

Prior to the drug epidemic in many areas, some gang groups generally financed their life-style through the commission of property offenses, such as robberies, auto thefts, and burglaries. This criminal activity still exists, but in the early 1980s, gangs became involved in street drug sales of cocaine, rock cocaine, PCP, and marijuana. Currently, rock cocaine is considered the primary drug sold in the streets by gangs.

Some older gang members, known as O.G.s or Original Gangsters, basically had ceased traditional gang activities and had gone into drug sales and distribution, using the younger members from their original gangs to sell the drugs on the streets. The older members were making substantial profits, and some were amassing large fortunes. They began to establish themselves as philanthropists, donating money to the areas where their gangs were from, and were soon known as "gang godfathers."

According to a 1990 report by the United States Department of the Treasury, a possible scenario of crack cocaine profit would be as follows:

- 75 crack houses operating in a city
- each house sells 50 grams daily (approximately 2 ounces)
- 75 houses × 50 grams each = 3,750 grams sold daily
- 3,750 grams = 3.75 kilograms
- profit on 1 kilogram = $88,000
- daily profit = $330,000
- yearly profit = $120,450,000

Due to high competition and the availability of rock cocaine, the price on the streets in many cities dropped significantly. In Los Angeles, the price of rock cocaine dropped significantly from $100 per gram during 1985-1986 to $20 to $30 per gram in 1987-1988.

Gang members began moving from Los Angeles to locate new markets to peddle their supplies of rock cocaine and PCP. They would send scouts to areas to investigate the possibilities of establishing a business. These scouts would provide free samples to some of the locals and then recruit them as dealers and members of the gang, and this would establish the newcomers in the community.

This strategy created a problem. The local dealers who were already doing business in that community saw the newcomers as a threat, and conflicts between these competitors soon began for the local business. Consequently, these conflicts resulted in an increase in violence and deaths in these cities. The reports indicate a pattern similar to that seen in such cities as Los Angeles.

As a result of these conflicts of power, many gangs aligned themselves not only with gangs who were traditional rivals but also with prison gang groups. They soon developed sophisticated organizations known for their violent criminal activity, in order to either gain or retain control of business in their areas.

Many law enforcement professionals compare this organized criminal activity to the Prohibition Era, where gangs and groups were in constant conflict and warfare for control of illegal activity and territories.

The Impact of Gangs and Drugs on Education

Many school systems have been experiencing an increase in gang-related activity, such as violence and drug dealing. As a result of this increase, many schools that usually had been patrolled by unarmed security officers are being forced to institute armed patrols. This requires funding equal to that of police officers, with costs for training, equipment, and support services.

One school district in Southern California recently asked for funding to hire nine additional police officers, police academy trained and armed at a cost of approximately $300,000, plus $20,000 for additional lighting for some of the schools.

There are many people who believe that it is not the school's responsibility to provide enforcement against the problems of violence and activity that the gang element produces. It is some people's belief that government or law enforcement agencies should deal with that problem, since that is what taxes are supposed to pay for. When this issue was presented to numerous educators and education administrators, their comments generally centered on the understanding that it is the school's responsibility to provide an environment that is safe and conducive to learning, for students and teachers, and that the police cannot always be available to deal with problems at schools. Therefore, there appears to be a need for armed security, which requires additional funding that is not usually available for that purpose, but could instead be used for educational purposes.

Many educators and law enforcement people believe that the parents should share in the responsibility to assist the schools in creating a safe environment. One major problem is that some parents have a laissez faire attitude toward their children's behavior away from home. Many times school administrators and teachers have this same attitude.

One county superintendent of schools in California indicated that the gang problem has hit some elementary, middle, and high schools severely. He described this gang problem as raw criminal activity, meaning illegal drugs, extortion, burglary, and assaults against students and teachers.

The schools can be considered a microcosm of the community and are a very vulnerable segment of the community. As one high school teacher describes it, many schools are becoming more violence prone than they have been because of the changing face of the community and the changes in the students. In early years, teachers knew the older brothers, sisters, and cousins of students. The teachers may have grown up with the parents. Their background was known, but now the new migration from tough urban areas has brought in a new and different type of students, with attitudes relevant to the urban schools. Some teachers believe they are a different kind of kid, in that they are used to resolving their conflicts through violence and they do not respect authority. They are not interested in school-sponsored activities, and sometimes their heroes or role models are criminal gangs or members. This idea is perpetuated by the tradition of family involvement. These kids understand the power of intimidation that identifying with a gang member provides when a person goes to a new school and community. This intimidation comes with styles of dress, which range from the traditional "gang type" dress to the current trend of wearing sports-logo clothing that in many cases relates to gang affiliation. The problem of dress codes and the impact it has in schools has become an issue that many view a violation of personal expression.

Costs to the Community

If the problem in the areas outside Los Angeles or other major urban areas is allowed to reach the same proportions as in Los Angeles, then those communities can expect a substantial drain on the local jurisdiction's resources. Law enforcement no longer considers street gang members small-time hoodlums, but a vital component of organized crime, demonstrating a propensity for violence. The result is an enormous pressure on law enforcement to control the activity, a pressure brought to bear by the increased outcry and demands by the community to "do something."

The cost of fielding a police officer at the entry level exceeds $52,000 per year, including benefits. Not included are the costs for equipment. With additional police officers, there is consequently an impact on support services, and a need for supervisors and more administrative help to properly support the increase in street-level operations. The impact affects other professionals: social services, district attorney's and public defender's offices, the courts, and many others who are impacted financially from the influx of gangs and their activity in the community. In one county in Southern California, the district attorney's office established a gang prosecution unit to deal specifically with the criminal activities of gangs. The estimated cost for the operation of this unit for one year is approximately $330,000. Another county, which was unable to obtain funding for that specific purpose, assigned two attorneys and one investigator to gang prosecution. They were taken away from other assignments without anyone replacing them. The basic thought is that a swift and aggressive response will be the only effective approach to combat gang problems. That response has a financial impact, at a very high cost to communities.

Another problem that creates a financial impact to communities that is directly related to gang activity is graffiti, known as the "newspaper of the streets." One city in Southern California has reportedly spent approximately 200 to 500 man-hours per month removing graffiti from public parks. The estimated cost to the taxpayers was reported to be between $3,000 and $4,000 per month, and that is only for salaries, not the cost of materials. That same community has been forced to lay off those workers as a result of budget constraints. Obviously, the gangs will see this as a victory, and the problem will only grow worse.

The problem with graffiti is that it has an impact on other aspects of the community. One school district in California spends approximately $1,700 per month removing graffiti, most of which is gang-related, on

57 school campuses. The cost of removing graffiti from private businesses and private property would be difficult to calculate, because the cost is not usually a matter of public record.

In addition to the graffiti that gangs leave in the community, a new phenomenon has surfaced, placing an added burden on the agencies that are trying to deal with defaced property. A new group of criminals, called "taggers," can be compared to the subway artists of New York and Chicago who paint subway cars, using multicolored patterns and signing them with unusual names ("tags") to identify their individuality. In California these "taggers" who have spread their artistry across the community have come to be viewed as destructive vandals with little or no concern for the property of others. They have formed themselves into groups with names depicting antisocial attitudes, which has created a form of rivalry and competitiveness against other "tagger" groups. Law enforcement has seen this new group of criminals slowly evolve into more traditional gang groups, becoming involved in shooting, painting over rivals' walls, wearing traditional gang clothing, and using terminology understood by very few people outside their groups. Law enforcement personnel are seeing a new trend among these "taggers," in that they now have become rivals to traditional street gangs, bringing on the element of violence against each other. This obviously intensifies the impact on communities already strapped for funding and services to help deal with gang-related activity.

Community Response

The most important ingredient to this effort on the war on gangs is the need to organize the community's participation along with that of the private sector. To accomplish this huge task, they all must be part of the law enforcement coalition.

It is my contention that the gang problem seen in communities throughout the country should be attacked by a diversified effort: suppression by law enforcement, diversions and intervention by community social service agencies, and education in schools for educators, students, parents, and the entire community. Many community programs provide services that combine diversion, intervention, and education.

The first element, suppression by law enforcement, is being attempted by many communities. They are training and utilizing special units to combat the gang and drug offenders, assisted by specialized prosecution units to ensure that they are dealt with swiftly and, of course, fairly.

S.M.A.S.H., the San Bernardino County Movement Against Street Hoodlums, is one such specialized unit, comprised of a combination of representatives from city police agencies from Riverside and San Bernardino counties. They work at gathering intelligence, sharing information on the gangs and gang members' activities, and any new trends that are constantly appearing. This group meets on a monthly basis and utilizes networking by all agencies to accomplish this objective. All information on individual gang members and associates is entered into a state-of-the-art computerized system known as G.R.E.A.T., Gang Reporting Evaluation and Tracking. This system has become so efficient that it is being used by criminal justice agencies nationwide.

In addition, S.M.A.S.H. is involved in unified training of personnel from all agencies. This ensures that any agency needing assistance will have access to not only a large pool of specialists to address the gang problem but also a disciplined and coordinated force to combat the problem.

One of the most important aspects of this special unit is its public relations and media relations program. This includes, but is not limited to, developing and coordinating gang awareness programs for the communities in Riverside and San Bernardino counties. A very important part of this effort is a 24-hour hotline for receiving information regarding any type of criminal activity. Callers may provide information anonymously, and may leave information so that an investigator can contact them at a later date.

Other units in effect are: the Los Angeles Police Department's C.R.A.S.H., Community Resources Against Street Hoodlums, and the Los Angeles County Sheriff's Department O.S.S., Operation Safe Streets. These are only a few of the Southern California agencies that are showing success in their operation. There are numerous cities with specialized units within their own departments that are successful, and that are an integral part of the combined units.

The second element for a community response is diversion, intervention, and prevention. The development of anti-gang programs has increased in many communities. Some address the prevention aspect, some are directed toward youths who are already involved in gang activity, while others have components that address a combination of strategies.

One such anti-gang program is the California Youth Authority's Gang Violence Reduction Project in Los Angeles. This program's main objective is to redirect youth gang members into positive activities. Strategies include mediation to resolve disputes between feuding gangs to prevent violence. In addition, gang members are encouraged to participate in organized recreational activities and social events. Recent additions are a suicide hotline, and an effort to assist youths who have quit school to attain their G.E.D. (General Education Development Certificate) through contracting teachers.

The Paramount Plan: Alternatives to Gang Membership, is part of the City of Paramount's Human Services Department. This program hires gang members as consultants to promote the project in their neighborhoods. It places an emphasis on the disapproval of gang membership, while attempting to both divert the future gang membership base and diminish gang influence. The strategies include sponsoring neighborhood meetings and providing anti-gang materials and posters upon request. A fifth-grade anti-gang curriculum was introduced in the Paramount Unified School District in 1982. This curriculum emphasized constructive activities available in the neighborhood. The Paramount Plan also includes an intermediate school follow-up program and an anti-gang family and individual counseling component. An additional second-grade gang-awareness curriculum was developed and began in 1990.

Another example of a prevention program is Vietnamese Community Orange County, Inc., in Santa Ana. This nonprofit organization consists of four programs to assist the Vietnamese community with a Youth Counseling and Crime/Drug Abuse Prevention Program. This component works in conjunction with prosecutors, educators, probation officers, and law enforcement officers to prevent Vietnamese youths from joining gangs. A youth counselor visits area schools and talks to students and guidance counselors, and also encourages parents to become involved in the programs. The organization offers English tutoring in addition to housing and employment services for refugees.

The element that may be the most difficult to accomplish is the involvement of the private sector. Youths involved in gangs need to be diverted into employment where they can gain work experience. Training and work experience are needed in high-risk areas where gangs recruit, because they would offer effective alternatives against gang participation, especially for the many youths involved in gangs that are considered "borderline." Communities can encourage the participation of private business and industry by going into economically depressed areas. Economic incentives could be provided to companies who employ workers from low-income areas. Of course, this is seen by many as unrealistic because there is a belief that gang members have no reason to work at entry-level jobs for entry-level wages when they could earn large amounts of money dealing drugs—a way of thinking that is difficult to overcome when the gangs have such an influence on these youths.

Conclusion

Neither the presence of gangs in the community nor the criminal activity they are involved in will be dissolved by police putting gang members in jail. Many times we hear that the root of the problem is economic issues, and in this case it is because a tremendous amount of money is earned through narcotics sales. It has become a way of life for many gang members. They may have been raised in homes by parents who either condone or have no knowledge of their children's activities. In many cases, the parents are also involved in that activity. It is believed that an entire generation is at stake here.

Generally speaking, the gang problem and the activities related to gangs are even more critical when the attitude of gang members is examined. Many do not have any respect for life or property, only money and status. They live without principles and no longer consider family, home, school, and church sacred.

Parents who place the responsibility on the traditional institutions to take care of their children need to be educated themselves. They need to become aware of the influences that our youths are exposed to and how the presence of these influences creates difficulties for them. Many problems in the family place these youths in a position to become easy prey for recruitment into gangs and drug use. On the other hand, many parents are busy working so they can provide their children with a standard of living they believe is necessary to prevent involvement in gangs and drugs. Consider the amount of time youths are away from home—at school, in the park, hanging out with friends—compared to how much time is spent as a family. It is no wonder that so many of our youths today choose the gangs as their "other family," when that "other family" is the one that can provide love, attention, recognition, excitement, adventure, and most of all, a feeling of being accepted for who they are no matter how they look or act. They can be part of a gang easier than part of a social group at school, which tends to be more relative to whether a person belongs in that group. The power of intimidation, a somewhat sick form of respect, is bestowed upon the gangs because of the way they dress and act, and their numbers provide an attraction.

Everyone is affected by the gang element in our community. No longer can we continue to say "That's not my problem, it only happens on that side of town, with those people." We can no longer remain in the state of denial on this problem. We need to recognize the impact that this denial will continue to have not only on our communities but also on this generation that is at stake. It is hoped that there will be some survivors from this cancer, for there will be many more casualties.

Reference

Martinez, F. B. (1988). *The impact of black gangs and drugs in the Inland Empire.* Pasadena: California Department of Youth Authority.

5

Public Policy Approaches to Alcohol-Related Problems

The Los Angeles County "Community Model"

AL WRIGHT

Purpose

This chapter synthesizes what has been written about the "social/community model" of alcoholism recovery and describes an "ideal" alcohol recovery program for Los Angeles County, termed the Community Recovery Center.

Philosophical Assumptions of the Program

The Community Recovery Center represents an alternative paradigm to the conventional treatment approaches that rely on the medical, clinical, or cage management models. The concepts, philosophy, and practices of Alcoholics Anonymous (AA) create the framework for the program. Two other philosophical assumptions are fundamental (Wright, 1987).

1. *Alcohol problems result from a reciprocal relationship between drinkers and their social environment.* This environment includes family, friends, the immediate community, and society in general. Problem drinking is, in part, a result of society's irrational attitudes and igno-

rance about alcohol. Problem drinking cannot continue without the support (albeit unintentional) of family, friends, co-workers, employers, and others in the drinker's social environment. Alcoholism is not an individual problem. The Community Recovery Center, therefore, does not focus treatment solely on the individual alcoholic—instead, it also attempts to overcome alcohol-related problems at the family and community levels. A positive sober environment is a crucial part of the program operation. This holistic view of alcoholism and recovery has important implications for the physical environment and activities of the Center.

2. *The foundations of recovery from alcoholism and other alcohol problems are the concepts of individual responsibility and experiential learning.* Recovering alcoholics learn through program experience to take responsibility for their own lives. The Community Recovery Center, therefore, does not see individuals as being passive recipients of treatment—instead, each person is believed to be actively responsible for his or her own recovery. People learn at the Center how to live non-alcoholic life-styles through the experience of solving day-to-day problems without resorting to alcohol as a coping mechanism.

These philosophical assumptions have important implications for program operations. There is a reciprocal relationship between the participants and the program staff: Helping others is as important to sustaining an individual's recovery as being helped. Life experience and personal qualities determine leadership and authority, whether the person is a newly sober alcoholic, a volunteer, or a professional counselor. Since everyone both gives and receives help, the distinctions between staff, volunteers, and program participants are not as clear as in conventional treatment programs with professional-client relationships.

The Community Recovery Center aims to restore to participants both their *function* and their *meaning* (see Dodd, 1986). Function allows resumption of social role, but meaning transforms the person. Participants are imbued with a sense of mission and destiny in fighting alcoholism—their own and that of others—and in this they transcend self and find purpose in life. The result is a feeling of warmth and empathy in the program, and enthusiasm among the individuals who have been empowered by the self-transcendent perspective and the mutual-aid process (see Frankl, 1984).

The scope of the Community Recovery Center is expanded beyond the identification and treatment of individual alcoholics. This extension results from a recognition that societal attitudes and practices regarding alcohol use are integral contributing factors to most alcohol-related problems. To address alcohol-related problems at the individual level more effectively, a simultaneous effort must also be made to reduce community denial of alcohol-related problems in the work, living, and social environments surrounding the drinker. It is equally important to recognize and address society's role in supporting inappropriate drinking behavior.

Program Activities

The Community Recovery Center, unlike a mutual self-help group, is a formal organization that provides staff and facilities to create a peer environment supportive of individual recovery decisions. Medical and counseling services are not provided. Participants are expected to select activities that are personally meaningful from a smorgasbord offering of social, recreational, educational, and supportive group activities. The common denominator among participants is a willingness to seek and offer assistance with an alcohol problem. Unless a specific target population is identified, services are made available to men and women of all ages, and to all ethnic and special population groups.

A wide variety of activities is made available by the Center—because recovery is a process that involves changing many aspects of one's life. Unstructured opportunities are provided to relax and meet people in a comfortable, alcohol-free setting. More structured activities range from relatively formal alcohol discussion and education groups, to strictly social and recreational events. Discussion and education groups cover a wide variety of topics, including the development of alcoholism, interpersonal relationships, parenting skills, self-esteem, stress reduction, women's issues, and other recovery-related concerns. Social and recreational activities range from an impromptu game of checkers to a dance, a card tournament, or a picnic open to the entire community. Center activities are often scheduled on evenings and weekends because these are frequently times when people have the strongest urge to drink.

Services also include assistance, either through counseling or referrals, in obtaining jobs, housing, legal assistance, psychological counseling, welfare benefits, and other needed help. Services at the Center are designed to be practical and pragmatic. Staff realize that after basic needs such as food, shelter, clothing, and an appropriate abstinent environment are met, numerous barriers to recovery may still exist for many individuals and target populations. Examples of such barriers are lack of job skills, illiteracy, civil or criminal legal problems, as well as medical, dental, and mental health problems (the list goes on and on). As a practical matter, it is appropriate to address some of these problems within the Center. In certain circumstances, it may be better to address these problems through a sophisticated referral network.

Recovery services include the provision of facilities where people with alcohol problems may participate in mutual self-help discussions and other service activities to reinforce their recovery. The Center may also offer service activities directed both toward the general community and to particular target groups in the community. It is an accessible resource to the community for information about alcohol-related issues, referrals to other alcohol services, and opportunities for volunteer activity.

Prevention

Prevention services include efforts by the Center to inform the public about alcohol problems and issues, to reinforce responsible social attitudes and policies regarding the appropriate use of alcoholic beverages, to instill in young people and other at-risk individuals positive values regarding alcohol consumption, and to reach out to people with alcohol problems and refer them to appropriate services. Emphasis is placed not only on chronic alcohol problems, but also on acute episodes, such as child and spousal abuse, driving under the influence, and other criminal activity.

Unlike conventional prevention efforts—which target individuals or groups of individuals—social/community model prevention also aims to intervene in public institutions and public policies. The objective is to reduce alcohol problems within the *entire community* of individuals by implementing appropriate environmental strategies and public policy initiatives. These prevention services attempt to increase community awareness about alcohol problems; educate community groups and service agencies about the effects of alcohol use; and involve the community in combating alcohol problems and supporting Center activities.

Community participation and support are essential to the survival of the Center. To encourage the community to take action concerning alcohol-related problems, the Center might solicit donations of supplies and equipment and ask for volunteers. Members of the community can also provide support in the form of donated services, fund-raising, and job opportunities for participants.

Program Facility and Social Environment

Program Facility

Because problem drinking is seen as resulting from interactions between persons and their environment, the Community Recovery Center pays as much attention to modifying the participant's social and physical environment as it does to helping the person work through his or her individual problems related to drinking. The physical environment of the Center is warm and homelike and, ideally, is located in a house rather than a hospital or medical building. There is sufficient space for a drop-in lounge area, large group meetings, and social events.

Social Environment

There are few barriers to entry or participation at the Center. The atmosphere is low-key and nonthreatening; there is a minimum of paperwork associated with program admission; fees are set in accordance with ability to pay; and there are few observable differences between staff and participants.

From the participant's point of view, entry into the Center is a very informal, friendly process; at most, it is a friendly chat. From the staff's perspective, however, what is taking place is an entrance interview. Information about the participant is being obtained—somewhat indirectly and over a period of time—that provides necessary background data about participants and their appropriateness for center admission.

There is little obvious paperwork. Staff may make some notes during or immediately after impromptu, informal conversations with participants. These notes are later expanded, from memory, to provide more detailed records.

Program Implementation

Volunteers are an essential part of the Community Recovery Center. They enhance the efforts of paid staff, thus enabling the program to provide a broad range of services cost-efficiently. Depending on their skills and interests, *volunteers can perform any of the functions of paid program staff.* Volunteers may lead or co-lead discussion and education groups, organize social and recreational events, help maintain and improve the Center facility, solicit funds and donations, make alcohol awareness presentations to community groups and service agencies, and assist in administrative tasks.

Volunteering also provides many opportunities to further the participant's own recovery through helping others to recover. Helping others can contribute to feelings of self-worth and purpose. Volunteers, many of whom are recovering, can be important role models for the newly sober. The Center encourages its participants to become alumni and volunteers in the program.

In its residential services, the Center relies heavily on peer support and peer pressure to help participants maintain sobriety. Residents play a major role in developing and enforcing house rules, determining who will be admitted and discharged, and helping one another deal with personal issues related to drinking. Residents are also instrumental in the day-to-day operation of the residence, including cooking, cleaning, laundry, and facility maintenance.

Program Accountability

The Community Recovery Center maintains participant records, which contain demographic information sufficient to identify individuals. These records satisfy data collection needs of the Center and also document compliance with the program service standards issued by the State Department of Alcohol and Drug Programs.

The *case management* approach generally used by "professional" alcoholism treatment programs does not fit the model used by the Community Recovery Center (see Borkman, 1988). Under case management, an individual professional (or team) assumes responsibility for meeting the needs of clients by linking them to recommended or required services suggested by their diagnosis. A detailed case file is maintained that consists of client name, identification number, diagnosis, problem, services rendered, and judgments about the client's progress. These records are often kept secret from the client, and only the case manager and supervisors have access to them. The case file symbolizes both the professional's control over the client and the client's dependency on the case manager for receiving services. It becomes a control mechanism in the agency for organizing and maintaining information about the client. It is also used by funding agencies and accrediting bodies to construct accountability and evaluation requirements for the agency.

The Community Recovery Center, by contrast, uses a *program management* approach. Rather than manage individual clients as cases, Center staff manage the physical and social environment of the facility. They help to develop and maintain an environment that is conducive to successful self-management and individual recovery. It is left to the participants to manage their own recovery, with help from recovering peers. The participant's major relationship is not with an individual case manager; instead, it is with recovering peers who have varying lengths of time and successful experience in being drug-free and having a new sober way of living.

Recovery and exit planning are viewed as an ongoing process, aimed at restoring meaning and function to the individual—not as a static written document to be kept in a case manager's file. Instead of collecting detailed individual records and written recovery and exit plans, the Center maintains compliance data as group records to document that the following services are being provided:

1. alcohol education
2. recovery and exit planning
3. individual and group sessions
4. participant involvement
5. recreational activities

Future Program Development

More empirical knowledge is needed about the operation of programs such as the Community Recovery Center. Also needed is publication of research findings, in a form regarded as legitimate by the mainstream alcohol treatment community.

The data collection system needs to be made more meaningful for evaluation of programs within the framework of the social/community model. This system needs to resolve the paradox and the inherent conflict in attempting to integrate programs based on these principles within a governmental system that is hierarchical and requires accountability for the use of public funds. Language and service agreements also are in need of further refinement to clearly define the expectations of funding sources, while still allowing programs the latitude necessary to operate according to social/community model principles. A more appropriate vocabulary needs to be developed to describe program objectives and outcomes.

Data systems and evaluative tools also are needed to measure the success of the Community Recovery Center in preventing alcohol-related problems and promoting recovery through changes in community attitudes and practices regarding drinking.

Specialized administrative and educational opportunities are needed to instruct staff about their roles and responsibilities in a peer-oriented setting. Currently, there are few formalized educational opportunities to learn about managing or working in social/community model programs. Most staff must rely on their personal experience in recovery and self-help groups. Although the creation and maintenance of an environment conducive to mutual self-help and peer support appears to be simple, it is in fact quite complex.

Equally challenging is the task of motivating communities to reevaluate their norms and standards about drinking. This requires the creation of a grass-roots social and political movement (see Mosher & Jernigan, 1988). The Community Recovery Center assists this effort by raising consciousness and facilitating coalition-building among a broad range of individuals and groups. These activities not only contribute to a necessary "critical mass" for achieving policy change, but the very process of organizing into a coalition provides a "sense of community power and ownership of the alcohol environment" (see Mosher & Jernigan, 1988).

Conclusion

The Community Recovery Center constitutes an approach to alcohol problems that is different in kind—not just different in degree—from a traditional clinical approach. While there is no research yet to show that services under the social/community model are more effective than traditional clinical services, there is nothing to demonstrate that they are any less effective. What the available research literature suggests is that, within very broad limits, all approaches are about equally effective.

A major advantage of the social/community model, however, is that it is more efficient. For a given amount of money, it is possible for the Community Recovery Center to reach a much larger number of people. This means that public monies for alcohol services may be used more efficiently by channeling more of these funds from clinical programs to those that follow the social/community model approach.

References

Borkman, T. (1988, August). *What are social model alcohol recovery programs?* Draft chapter for textbook on social model principles (Sandra Shaw, Ed.).

Dodd, M. D. (1986, February). *What does social model mean?* Paper presented at University of California, San Diego, conference on California's Social Model of Recovery From Alcoholism, San Diego.

Frankl, V. E. (1984). *Man's search for meaning: An introduction to logotherapy* (3rd ed.). New York: Simon & Schuster.

Mosher, J., & Jernigan, D. (1988, Spring). Public action and awareness of alcohol-related problems: A plan of action. *Journal of Public Health Policy, 9*(1), 17-41.

Wright, A. (1987, November) *California's social model: A brief history and statement of basic concepts.* Paper presented at a conference of the American Public Health Association, Boston.

PART III

Prevention and Intervention Strategies

6

The Impact of Gang Violence

Strategies for Prevention and Intervention

LISA PORCHÉ-BURKE
CHRISTOPHER FULTON

> Her arm nearly severed by a shotgun blast, a 13 year old Long Beach girl begged in vain for mercy before gang members fired several more shots that claimed her life. . . . They executed her for nothing. . . . They wanted to kill something, so they killed her.
>
> Abrahamson & Malnic, 1991[1]

Introduction

Of the dozens of scientific journal articles on gangs and gang violence, only a few discuss prevention or intervention programs. Authors tend to describe the negative impacts gangs have on our society; some may postulate reasons that adolescents join gangs; but only a few propose specific prevention methods for addressing this issue. This chapter will attempt to discuss the myriad factors contributing to gang membership and violence by presenting three theories of why individuals join gangs, followed by a review of current prevention and intervention models

85

designed to address these issues, and finally recommendations regarding a more appropriate approach for dealing with gang violence.

Gang activity can no longer be conceptualized as isolated events occurring in the hub of urban centers. Survey results indicate an increase in prevalence of gang violence in small cities and towns (Miller, 1981). Gangs are formed in a wide variety of areas and impact most socioeconomic classes and ethnic groups (Roper, 1991). Destructive gang activity includes defacement of property, impediments to the population (especially those who are naive about turfs and trying to cross them), intimidation of local businesses, presence of community fear and anxiety, and a general destruction of community life (Spergel, 1984). There are high costs to the community in property damage, carnage of innocent victims, theft and robbery of local businesses, and drug trafficking. In Los Angeles alone, there have been more than 5,000 reported crimes each year for the past 3 years that are gang-related (Gates, 1990). Police Chief Gates reported that there were 1,112 drive-by shooting incidents resulting in 1,675 victims. Furthermore, crime reports in Los Angeles indicate that more than 68% of arrests of gang members are for felony charges (California State Task Force on Gangs and Drugs, 1989). In Los Angeles one of four homicides in 1988 was gang-related (Donovan, 1988). Police reports indicate that approximately 50% of victims of gang activity have no association with gangs whatsoever. The California Senate Committee on Children and Youth (1975) contends that innocent bystanders get victimized when crossing a territory made by a gang. According to the California State Task Force on Gangs and Drugs (1989), there are between 600 and 650 gangs, constituting more than 70,000 members, in the Greater Los Angeles area. Also, according to the California Senate Committee on Children and Youth (1975), increased mobility, access to handguns and machine guns, and increased drug trafficking have accelerated gang violence and spread its impact to neighboring communities.

Violent and/or criminal behavior is thought to be reinforced by peer pressure within the gang. Power within the gang subculture is obtained by both money (through drug sales or robbery) and the number of violent acts committed. These acts of violence and criminal activity demonstrate a member's allegiance to the gang and ability to carry out such acts. Often, initiation into gangs requires an illegal or violent act (e.g., a drive-by shooting or stealing from a homeowner). Also, recruitment into gangs often involves coercion or intimidation. Adolescent and prepubescent boys and girls fear being "jumped," and thus join gangs as a necessity, to keep from being harmed. A simple event like walking home from school requires seeking protection from gang intrusions or assaults. Thus, violence in America continues to jeopardize the lives of our youths and impair the quality of life in the communities where they reside (Wilson-Brewer & Jacklin, 1991). When one recognizes the severity of this problem, it is a natural step to look for theoretical explanations for its existence. The next section will address three theoretical conceptualizations of why individuals may seek gang membership.

Theories of Gang Violence

There are several popular explanations of why adolescents join gangs. From a theoretical perspective the *Opportunity Theory*, the *Disorganization Theory*, and the *Subculture Theory* are three such explanations of the lure of gang membership (Thompson & Jason, 1988). The Opportunity Theory asserts that individuals experience frustration due to the lack of opportunity to reach goals through conventional means. This theory stems from previously formulated strain theories that go back to the '50s and '60s (Cloward & Ohlin, 1960; Cohen, 1955). Hagedorn (1988) argues that because of technological advances in industry, there is an underclass created by a drastic reduction in the demand for manufacturing jobs requiring unskilled and semiskilled workers. This underclass, largely consisting of people of color, is locked out of the labor market, thereby blocking its upward mobility (Wilson, 1987). Even previous alternative career opportunities for the poor, such as the military, are less available due to the higher quality of applicants generated by an economy with relatively few attractive entry-level positions for unskilled workers (Huff, 1989). Hence, supporters of this theory contend that institutionalized racism is a distinct agent facilitating this denial of opportunity for people of color. Systemic oppression denies people of color freedom of expression, upward mobility, job opportunities, and a variety of elementary choices that many members of the majority culture take for granted. Thus, gang activity is thought to be a reaction to a discriminating and dominant middle class, which prevents the gang members from having access to opportunities while at the same time exposing them to middle-class aspirations and values (Fox, 1985). There are endless examples of discrimination in our society, but illustrating such cases is beyond the scope of this chapter. Denial of opportunities happens in all areas of the hierarchical structure, ranging from institutional to individual expressions of oppression.

A closely related hypothesis to the Opportunity Theory is the Disorganization Theory, which is gaining more acceptance among researchers. This theory attempts to explain that it is the community and family disarray that contributes to gang violence. It states that disorganization of family and local institutions accounts for the development of violent gangs (Kornhauser, 1978; Spergel, 1984). Hence, some theorists assert that schools, local communities, ethnic organizations, and local businesses fail to provide adequate mechanisms for increased opportunities and socialization to the values of the dominant culture. Spergel (1984) argues that gangs have become an alternate source of income, as well as a status-producing structure. It is argued therefore that gangs also provide a structure for the socialization of young adults in light of the breakdown in the familial institution's and other secondary institutions' ability to do so. Conversely, Tolan (1988) contends that lower levels of deviant behavior occur in more cohesive and supportive families as well. Family cohesion depends upon the family's ability to sufficiently communicate and supervise; parental presence in the home; and the family's ability to resolve conflict (Patterson, DeBaryshe, & Ramsey, 1989). Thus some authors postulate that adequate family socialization can be achieved if youths have the opportunity to be involved in activities, if they develop skills necessary to be successfully involved, and if the appropriate behaviors are consistently rewarded by family and community members (Hawkins & Weis, 1985). When deterioration in the family socialization process occurs, gang membership provides the necessary nurturance that the family lacks. Often youths feel loved, respected, and supported for the first time as a result of joining a gang. Fellow gang members will risk their life for the new member and find much honor in dying for a fellow gang member. Thus, gang membership helps individuals meet certain personal needs, such as expression of oneself, security, group identity, organization in a group, social interaction, and status.

In earlier writings, Suttles (1968) asserted that gangs originated to protect new immigrants and community settlers because of law enforcement's inability to do so. This theory, referred to as the Subculture Theory, holds that gang behavior and membership are not viewed as deviant within a given subculture. This is clearly supported by researchers evaluating community tolerance to gang activity (Horowitz, 1987). Horowitz found that gang members are not considered outsiders, but are in fact members of family networks in which the specific behaviors associated with gang membership are regarded as appropriate. Often community members tolerate gang membership by avoiding direct awareness of the violent acts of their sons and daughters and/or aligning such acts with cultural standards of honor. Horowitz (1987) asserts that the social structure will continue until violent confrontations disrupt community affairs, such as dances or weddings. This failure is also noted in the implications that asserted the existence of family involvement in violent activities. Only during these two instances did the collaboration and maintenance of social order between gang members and their family or community crumble. There are several current societal contributors to gang membership and violence. Spergel (1984) suggests that immigrant flow and resettlement, racism, housing segregation, unemployment, lack of economic resources, and access to handguns should be conceived as national level contributors to gang violence, and therefore, they warrant our serious attention. He also outlines several local problems, such as weak community organizations, lack of young adult bridging mechanisms, and unsystematic police strategies, as additional contributors to this issue. Other possible factors that have been suggested to be causative in the gang violence problem include an increase of importation of drugs into the United States; the growth of the so-called underclass and the alienation of this underclass; and cutbacks in state-funded and federally funded job, drug, recreation, and educational programs (Donovan, 1988). Clearly, however, just looking at why individuals join gangs is not an adequate response. The rising statistics of violent outbursts in our communities mandate that we not only understand what a gang is but also that we look seriously to how we as a nation of people can begin to address this deadly problem.

The Definition

While gangs include many people, coming from various ethnic, socioeconomic, and age groups, gang members tend to congregate within their "territory," which usually includes their homes, schools, and local communities. Morash (1983, p. 309) states that gangs are "structured according to age, have a well-defined leadership, and engage in a wide range of activities together." Criminologists in Los Angeles have divided the street gangs into two broad categories: cultural gangs and instrumental gangs (Sessions, 1990). According to

Sessions, cultural gangs are described as neighborhood-centered and exist independently of criminal activity. In Los Angeles the two main cultural gangs are predominantly African-American and Hispanic, although there are rising numbers of Asian-Pacific gangs (Donovan, 1988; Sessions, 1990). Conversely, instrumental gangs are formed for the purpose of carrying out criminal acts, and pose a greater threat than cultural street gangs because they are highly organized (Sessions, 1990). It has further been suggested that gangs previously defined as cultural gangs developed into instrumental gangs because of their involvement with interstate organized crime and drug trafficking. For example the Crips and Bloods, predominantly African-American street gangs in Los Angeles, are known to have direct contact with major drug importers and to use Southern California as a major cocaine transshipment point.

There are numerous definitions of a gang. While some broad definitions would include car clubs and college fraternities, other more narrow and restrictive ones would be exclusive to street gangs. Some researchers have supported a narrow definition of a gang, suggesting it is two or more individuals who: (a) associate on a continuous basis; (b) claim a name and territory; and (c) engage collectively or individually in a criminal activity that directly or indirectly benefits the gang (Donovan, 1988). Although Donovan's definition attempts to encompass a variety of types of gangs, while simultaneously excluding legitimate groups, it assumes the term *gang* has a negative connotation and that gangs, in and of themselves, are destructive. In Donovan's definition, gangs necessarily include violence and criminal activity. Researchers have found that gang membership itself is not a sufficient condition to stimulate delinquency or violence (Downes, 1966; Morash, 1983). A more narrow and restrictive definition of a gang allows for only narrow methods of addressing gang violence. Hence, it is our belief that by incorporating a broader definition of gangs and gang violence, we can develop and implement more diverse methods of approaching the problem of gang violence in our communities.

Characteristics of a Gang Member

It is often believed that there is a specific personality or character that is prone to gang membership. It is suggested that adolescents with conduct disorders or who are oppositional and defiant tend to be attracted to gangs. Undisputedly, many gang members engage in violent acts, and most are defiant toward authority figures, but these explanations of gang membership address the result, not necessarily the cause. We cannot answer the question of whether an adolescent was defiant before or after joining a gang. Also, less blaming attributes appear to be more useful in helping to depict individuals who are potential gang members. Lack of identity, lack of education, lack of job skills, and lack of social skills are a few such attributes. It seems simplistic only to attribute the lack of such abilities to the individual, and we would indeed be falling prey to the construct of "blaming the victim." Clearly, if we are to seriously address these issues, it is up to the community and its institutions to provide training opportunities to develop marketable skills, adequate socialization experiences for teenagers, educational opportunities for youngsters, a stable and predictable environment, and a sense of commonality.

Previously, gang members were typically thought to be older persons and new immigrants to the country (California Senate Committee on Children and Youth, 1975). But today gang members are younger, permanent United States citizens, from a broad spectrum of ethnic/cultural backgrounds, and they are perceived as more dangerous. For instance, we know that there is a considerable number of Asian-Pacific gangs who are organized, have drug connections in their native countries, are highly mobile, and have a substantial financial surplus (California Senate Committee on Youth and Children, 1975; California State Task Force on Gangs and Drugs, 1989; Donovan, 1988). What we also know is that among youths between the ages of 15 and 24, homicide is the second leading cause of death, surpassed only by unintentional injuries (Roper, 1991). This picture becomes even more stark when we look at the statistics emerging out of our ethnic communities. Within these communities, we see that homicide rates among young African-American males are seven to eight times higher than among white males, that Hispanic and Native American males' homicide rate is four to five times higher than that of white males, and that, more specifically, the leading cause of death among African-American youths is homicide (Roper, 1991). Thus we have a grim picture that describes our youths, and in particular our ethnic youths, at high risk for involvement in gang-related problems. This is the reality we face today. These are not just statistics. These youths are *our* future. Clearly, we must, as a society take active steps in addressing this growing problem. We must look toward prevention as well as intervention aspects of this problem if we are to truly address the magnitude of this issue in our communities. The next section

of this chapter will look at some of the prevention/intervention strategies that have been used to address this growing problem of gang
violence.

Current Prevention and Intervention Methods

A review of the literature suggests current methods of gang intervention
and prevention include primarily the following: (a) law enforcement; (b)
some social institutions/programs; and (c) a few community-based
programs.

Law Enforcement

It is argued here that although law enforcement has an important role
in gang violence intervention, the role of a police officer needs to be
broadened to involve more interaction with the community. We agree
with the notion of a community-based intervention program, but argue
that the police need to become a part of the community, rather than its
disengaged patroller. Many police forces are currently expanding the
role of officers by placing them back on the beat (Lacayo, 1991). This
assignment requires officers to patrol a designated neighborhood on
foot. Lacayo maintains that officers on this assignment become intimately acquainted with the members of the community, which enables
the officers to build a rapport with them. Seeing positive aspects of the
community has a reciprocative effect on police and their reaction to
community members, removing the "enemy image" of out-group members. This in turn will preclude overly aggressive behavior directed
toward gang members, which is typically reciprocated with vengeance
from the gang itself. Huff (1989) found that gang members appreciate
"fair" treatment and respond favorably by respecting the officer. This
is especially true if the officer shows any concern for the gang members;
for instance, if the officer asks how they are doing or knows any history
about them. Huff stated that, "Gang members admitted grudgingly
respect for police who acted professionally and demonstrated some
personal concern" (p. 531).

If law enforcement is more involved with the community, the officers
find themselves preventing crime before it occurs, rather than their
usual assignment of apprehending the criminal after the crime has been
committed. For example, officers once closed an abandoned building

that was used for drug dealing after discovering it during the arrest of a local drug dealer (Huff, 1989). Therefore, it is suggested here that this type of community involvement is needed to establish cooperative and meaningful relationships between the police and community members, which is imperative to gang violence prevention. Having such community support and involvement would instill feelings of confidence and appropriate authority, which it is hoped would reduce the need for using excessive force in interacting with or detaining gang members. Simultaneously, there is hope that having community involvement would counterbalance the feeling of lacking impact because of our cumbersome judicial system and the difficulty in convicting criminals (Lacayo, 1991). An important and critical ingredient to the proposed involvement of police is the training of officers to understand the cultural and ethnic composition of the communities they patrol. Without this level of understanding, no intervention will be truly successful.

One of the foremost problems with the reliance on law enforcement is that responsibility is not shared. Communities displace their responsibility onto the police, depending on them to rid the community of its problems. Law enforcement has responded by expanding its gang-control functions, including intelligence and investigation agencies. In Los Angeles County, a special police unit, called Operation Safe Streets, as well as an extensive information-gathering system, have been established to control gang violence (McBride & Jackson, 1989). The officers contend that "if any real progress can be made to secure society against gangs and drugs, it will have to be through the use of sophisticated, specialized, law enforcement units trained in combating them and through the newer tools technology makes available to us" (p. 31). However, McBride and Jackson acknowledged law enforcement's limitation in addressing problems of gang violence, supporting the development of community-based prevention programs. There has been a public health effort in prevention of gangs in response to the realization that the prevention of violence is beyond the capabilities of the criminal justice system acting alone (Cohen & Lang, 1991).

Social Programs: Prevention and Intervention Examples

Social services refer to myriad efforts for assisting people in their day-to-day social activities and promoting collective social life (Shannon, 1983). Shannon exposes several shortcomings of our current social services system, using social welfare as the prime example of a direct intervention. Social services often have unclear goals and priorities, are powerless at the local level, suffer from bureaucratic inertia, have poor coordination, and suffer from rising costs. These problems prevent social agencies from implementing adequate programs. Thus, there is a failure to address community-specific needs since the managing of such programs is done from distant headquarters (Shannon, 1983). It is clear that there needs to be a decentralization of power to facilitate more responsiveness on the part of social agencies, which could then have a reciprocal effect in allowing such agencies to be more responsive.

Some of the lack of responsiveness lies within the training of the social agency's staff. Many social institutions fail to impact communities who have identifiable gang members because even well-intentioned social workers lack the training needed to address issues of cultural diversity and gangs (Fox, 1985). Most social workers have been white, middle-class individuals who receive training from a dominant cultural framework. This biased and difficult training, combined with the facts that many gang members are people of color and that gangs themselves are a subculture, leads to a less-than-perfect interaction. Furthermore, many otherwise competent social workers refuse to work in poor or dangerous neighborhoods (Fox, 1985), motivated by a genuine concern for safety and/or racist views. There are legitimate concerns for safety in certain areas, but it is speculated here that many individuals refuse to work with specific ethnic or gang populations. Fox outlines a 6-stage model of a community intervention program, similar to the one used by the Central Harlem Street Clubs Project. Applying a direct intervention strategy to present-day gang problems, Fox's model includes: (1) contact, (2) rapport, (3) setting goals, (4) assigning roles, (5) procuring resources, and (6) evaluation. The model relies on a "detached worker," an individual who is based more in the immediate environment or community rather that in the agency's office. This is a similar approach to that discussed earlier regarding a different type of police effort for developing more prevention activities. It is recommended here that the social agency's interventions be intimately interwoven with the police, establishing a cooperative, integrative working relationship. This will in fact alleviate some of the safety concerns for the community worker, involve officers more with the community, help maintain well-informed officers, and establish a team effort that taps additional resources.

Stage one of Fox's model, *contact*, requires the community worker to overcome any aversion or defensiveness to interacting with gang members and people of color. Fox did not describe the training process in detail, although it included addressing issues of diversity. We believe that training around the community interventions for gang violence and substance abuse should include: (a) education on issues of cultural diversity; (b) communication skills building; (c) acquiring flexible worldviews; (d) instruction on de-escalation skills; and (e) identifying real versus imagined danger. Spergel (1984) suggested that social workers should become well trained in crisis intervention so they can help resolve different kinds of disputes, including gang versus police, gang versus community, and intergang disputes.

Stage two, *rapport*, involves breaking through cultural and communication barriers while attempting to build an honest and open relationship with gang members. Fox's model points out that this is particularly difficult because of the alienation, distrust, and defensiveness common among gang members. The third stage, *setting goals*, determines the course and duration of the working relationship with gang members. Fox notes not only the difficulty in coming up with agreed upon goals but also that sometimes the relationship must be terminated at this point. Gang members are often frustrated with this part of the process because previously their goals were frequently blocked by the community and by individuals. Although Fox suggests that community concerns be considered, it is urged here that community members be involved with this process in an effort to better define issues that need to be addressed and to allow community members to hear the concerns of gang members directly. The fourth step is *assigning roles*, which Fox describes as particularly difficult since gang members often expect direct help once they have identified their needs and goals. Thus, Fox proposes that responsibilities be divided and roles be assigned as democratically as possible after goals have been agreed upon. Again, it is recommended here that communities be involved with this part of the process, involving assigning and receiving roles, in working toward the agreed upon goals. It is contended here that community involvement will communicate to the gang members that gang and substance abuse problems are being heard and that people have concern and a dedication to the amelioration of problems associated with gang violence and substance abuse. The fifth stage, *procuring resources*, involves the social worker's helping to develop more adaptive talents to modify the image of the gang held by the community, as well as to develop benefits for the youths themselves. Resources should be procured by gang members themselves, by community programs, and by local institutions. The final stage involves *evaluating the results*, and it is thought that the primary evaluation should come from the gang members themselves. It is recommended here that the community members take a leading role in this evaluation process as well, since the community is directly impacted by gang violence and substance abuse and its members will often have to continue control over such problems themselves. The community and its members must remain after the intervention. Thus, the community can and should play a vital role in sustaining intervention designed to address gang-related problems. Community members should continue to meet with gang members, social institutions, and police in an effort to continue the maintenance of ameliorating the problem.

In reviewing intervention programs, we found that most attempts include assisting youths in developing what are considered "appropriate" social relationships and behavior (Thompson & Jason, 1988). Thompson and Jason contend that intervention methods "must provide opportunities for involvement in conventional activities, interaction with conventional others, and the application of requisite skills that make the involvement and interaction rewarding" (p. 325).

Direct intervention strategies, however, impact a problem *after* it has occurred, but in fact do not *prevent* the problem from occurring in the first place. Thus, a focus on prevention is critical if we are to get a handle on the growing problems associated with gang violence. Public health efforts have drastically increased in the past decade, with an intense focus on the prevention of violence in our communities. Several prevention programs that appear to demonstrate some efficacy for a comprehensive approach to gang violence will be discussed here in an effort to underscore the importance of prevention strategies attacking this issue. One such prevention effort is currently in place in the Los Angeles area. The largest non-law-enforcement anti-gang program in the country is the California Youth Gang Services Project. Funding for the program comes from the City and County of Los Angeles, the State of California, Department of Health and Human Services, United Way, and the Los Angeles Police Department. The program is aimed at crisis intervention, mobilizing the community, prevention, parent-teacher education, job development, and graffiti removal. Its comprehensive prevention methodology includes education through seminars, pamphlets, and classes. The classes assist youths in identifying negative aspects of joining a gang, and inform teachers and parents on how to identify high-risk youths and what measures to take in preventing them from joining gangs and using drugs. One of the educational programs is a

"Career Paths Program," a 15-week course that teaches about the negative aspects of gangs and promotes positive alternatives to the lure of gang membership. Los Angeles police claim that the program is working well in targeted South-Central Los Angeles areas, announcing a 67% drop in gang-related drive-by shootings in the area, a 10% reduction in street crimes, and a 14% decline in school truancy (Holguin, 1991). A problem with this program is its link with the police, which removes much of its credibility. Also, being tied with the police, the program lacks creativity in its approach to curbing gang violence. For instance, it is suggested by the authors that schools be encouraged to include culturally appropriate curricula rather than educate youth in a traditional fashion. Although imperfect, programs like this that possess adequate funding, community implementation, and a comprehensive approach are needed to sufficiently prevent gang violence.

Another Violence Prevention Project has been implemented in Boston, Massachusetts, as part of the Health Promotion Program for Urban Youth, Boston Department of Health and Hospitals. This community-based program has both primary and secondary prevention components, which aim at changing individual behavior and community attitudes about violence (Prothrow-Stith, 1991). The intervention includes a 10-session violence prevention curriculum used in the high schools and in other settings, such as Sunday schools and boys' and girls' clubs. The program is designed "to provide descriptive information on the risks of violence and homicide, provide alternative conflict resolution techniques, and create a classroom ethos that is nonviolent and values violence-prevention behavior" (Prothrow-Stith, 1991, p. 238). The program can be modified as appropriate to fit the youths it is attempting to reach. Currently the project is concentrating its efforts in Boston's two poorest neighborhoods. Additionally, the project has expanded its efforts to reach youths who are admitted to the Boston City Hospital with intentional injuries.

There are currently a variety of educational programs sponsored by various institutions and agencies. The Los Angeles police department sponsors DARE (Drug Abuse Resistance Education), a program that educates elementary and middle-school-aged children about the negative effects of drugs and gangs (Pierce & Ramsay, 1990). Although a program such as this is vital in a comprehensive approach to preventive measures against gang violence and drug problems, this program is often unsuccessfully relied upon as the only method of intervention.

Parent education is currently being implemented by many law enforcement agencies as well. For instance, in Los Angeles County the police have been involved with a parent educational program, Parents Against Gang Entrapment (PAGE), which is aimed at educating parents about youth gangs and providing a support system for parents of gang members (Pierce & Ramsay, 1990). PAGE is not directly affiliated with the police, but police both inform parents of their children's gang activity, recommending that they attend PAGE meetings, and request information from parents about gang activity in their neighborhood. Although half the parents notified of their children's gang activity often deny such allegations, many parents take an active role in learning about gang problems, become familiar with the signs of gang activity, and learn how to keep their child from becoming further involved with gang violence and drugs (Pierce & Ramsay, 1990).

Summary of Issues and Recommendations

There is an abundance of biases and problems with current intervention programs and their assumptions. The authors repeatedly use terms like *conventional* and *appropriate*. This line of thought assumes that gang activity, in and of itself, is wrong, rather than some of its violent manifestations. To whom are social problems a problem? Typically, it is those outside the boundaries of a given social condition who define social problems. There aren't intervention and prevention programs for white-collar criminal activity, although this type of crime costs much more than typically publicized violent crimes (Shannon, 1983). As our society becomes more conservative, people tend to favor intra-psychic as opposed to environmental roots to social problems. Clearly, the definition of a problem determines the approaches used in finding solutions. Consequently, attempts are made at influencing, controlling, or changing high-risk populations, which forces them to conform to mainstream culture. Additionally, if a high-risk population member does participate in the majority's activities, he or she must at least act in a nonintrusive, conforming manner.

There are numerous current shortcomings and biases in the methods of defining and addressing social problems. Seidman (1986, p. 237) suggest that "the social scientist in collaboration with representatives of the judicial and crime control organizations agree, often unwittingly and usually for unexpressed reasons, to solve some problem before they have considered it the 'right' problem." Seidman asserts that this situation increases the likelihood, without notice, of selecting the "wrong" problem. Many current program researchers contend that if social agencies simply teach conventional methods of attaining goals, the potential gang member will not join street gangs. But what happens when this individual, often a person of color, realizes that the dominant culture won't allow him or her to attain such goals, despite his or her acculturating to white norms? It is our contention that this is why gangs are created. In short, they assist individuals in acquiring power, achieving goals, and establishing a sense of identity, not otherwise attainable in either a community setting or the current structure of our society. Inherent in this is the fatal flaw of focusing on changing *only* the individual rather than both the individual and the system he or she is a part of. The person can change, but if the system is not designed to accommodate this, individuals will continue to utilize unconventional means to obtain goals. Thus, until *realistic* goals are established, the strength and purpose of gangs are identified, and the community makes adjustments, no long-lasting change can be achieved. In fact, by the mere implementation of many of our current intervention programs, we have participated in institutionalized racism through our attempts to control or influence gangs (who are comprised of high-risk populations, or those outside the boundaries of the group defined as the problem) without truly understanding the nature of the problem. Seidman (1986, p. 244) states this is especially true for our correctional system: "Placement in a behavior modification program maintains the representatives of authority in a position of dominance and concomitantly keeps the prisoner in his/her place, that is, down, but more systematically and effectively." Seidman suggests that such programs reinforce, rather than change, the ingrained feelings of powerlessness and the actions that may lead a person to commit future criminal acts. We view gang activity as a response to oppression; it serves many important purposes, most notably, providing a sense of identity and power. Stripping membership from a gang member would be like a clinician removing a client's defense mechanism, with the result being an exposed individual who lacks many of the necessary coping skills to survive in our society.

There are numerous problems with relying solely on law enforcement and/or specific social agency programs. Spergel (1984, p. 221) points out two paramount problems with these current intervention measures:

[I]ncreased deterrence may result in a higher rate of arrests and imprisonment and subsequently increased criminal behavior of gang members because of exposure to the justice system and penal experience. Simple "dogoodism" or provision of opportunities through the gang structure may result in capture and manipulation of resources and services, resulting in increased criminal activity by the gang and the development of sophisticated gang organization.

Therefore, a comprehensive and multiphase, multilevel program is suggested here—one that involves changes in both the community and law enforcement as well as identifying programs that will directly address issues of opportunity, power, and status for the youths who seek to get there via gang membership. Social institutions should assist in the facilitation of preventative efforts, but should acknowledge their limitations in making lasting changes without the community's maintaining such efforts.

It is suggested that the answer lies in a more comprehensive perspective. Programs must be community-based, bringing together the police, schools, council members, and local businesses. The programs will meet the specific needs of the community, rather than forcing community members into a framework that does not work. Often the community itself knows what problems need to be addressed and how to address them. Community members can provide vital information about how oppression, lack of local job opportunities, and anomie impact and affect its youths.

Why Community-Based Programs?

While it is generally agreed upon that there is a gang violence and drug problem, differences lie in the definition of and method of addressing the problem. According to the California State Task Force on Gangs and Drugs (1989), most community members, justice personnel, and law enforcement recognize the inability to contain gang violence strictly through the criminal justice system. The Task Force stated: "Representatives from community organizations, service agencies, and criminal justice entities stressed the overriding need for long-term solutions to the gang and drug problem through prevention and intervention programs." Even the police force recognizes its limitations in providing a solution to gang violence. Los Angeles Police Chief Daryl F. Gates maintains that prevention programs are the best remedy to gang violence, but that it will take much time before results will be noticeable (Gates, 1990).

It is suggested here that cities employ a community-based gang intervention program, utilizing local schools, religious organizations, businesses, law enforcement, and federal agencies. A prominent community member or leader should be the mediator between the different institutions and should facilitate communication and mutual cooperation. The local government can play an instrumental role in assisting the execution and funding of such programs. But these officials should not be solely relied upon since there is often much self-interest in gaining political advantage, rather than meeting the needs of the community members. Community members have the most insight and influence on local problems. This influence can be used to establish a successful mentor program, utilizing role models from local businesses, athletes, government officials, clergy, and former gang members. The mentors must come from various ethnic backgrounds to better represent the population being targeted. A demonstration of a community-based program using its power constructively can be seen in Los Angeles's Community Youth Gang Services Project. According to the California State Task Force on Gangs and Drugs (1989), the staff of this project often intercedes in potentially volatile situations and counsels gang members in conflict resolution techniques. Some of the first steps that need to be taken by community members involve making contact with and building rapport with gang members. This should be followed by goal setting, which should not be done in an overly compromising fashion. To achieve adequate goals the community interventions should request information from gang members about what membership provides for them and how violence and substance abuse can be avoided. Also, the leaders can educate youths on how gang membership negatively impacts them (i.e., how it takes away many freedoms and actually may increase the possibility of being jumped). It is suggested here that gang members and youths who are potential gang members be educated and trained, utilizing their strengths. It is imperative, however, that education and training be done in a supportive rather than demeaning way. Educators should take precautions in how the training is approached, avoiding any implication that the intervener perceives himself or herself as morally superior. Local businesses can inform workers which skills and training are necessary to receive employment and can participate in the actual training as well. Schools can also be called upon to develop creative methods of teaching that address many of the problems and stigmas associated with formal education. The education system has lost much of its legitimate power, undermining the socialization process that is expected of it (Shannon, 1983). Responsiveness needs to be encouraged through a decentralization of authority, thus enabling community members to establish specific programs that meet the needs of the children in the community. Spergel (1984) suggests that programs should be aimed at increasing community cohesion and strengthening institutions' abilities in facilitating socialization. Measures should be taken to assist various neighborhood groups and organizations in becoming more responsive with respect to the needs of gang youth for education, training, jobs, drug rehabilitation, family counseling, and other services. Also, Spergel suggests that communities enlist former gang leaders as role models and educators for teaching about viable and more adaptive alternatives to gang membership. Setting up a program such as this, rather than a social agency based program, establishes a long-standing solution, not a temporary one. Agencies run out of funding and change staff frequently, but the schools, businesses, and community members are more permanent elements of the community.

The community-based program needs to be implemented in such a way that possible obstacles are anticipated and dealt with as needed. One of the reasons why gang problems are not adequately addressed is that law enforcement, public services, and community agencies may use gang information to further their political or organizational goals (Donovan, 1988). Often these goals will not coincide with those of the community, which is most directly impacted by gang violence and drug problems. Donovan also outlines another problem: Community leaders, school administration, and local politicians may deny gang problems for fear of offending ethnic communities or stigmatizing school districts or neighborhoods. And finally, gang and drug problems are often considered by white mainstream public opinion as the exclusive problem of a particular ethnic population or community. Thus, a community-based program is needed because it will be the most responsive to the community's needs and will circumvent denial of any problem. Also, prevention programs such as these are much less costly than indirect and direct impacts of crime, rehabilitation, and correction (Klein, 1969).

The community needs to accept partial responsibility for promoting gang-related problems, as well as curing the problems. It is necessary for the community to identify such problems, set short-term tangible goals, and utilize the resources needed to address them. Ultimately, the community needs to provide for its youths the means for developing a healthy identity, and that includes resources, training, education, adequate socialization, and the establishment of open lines of communication. It is believed that change in an individual is facilitated by the group to which that person belongs (Sheerer, 1985). Thus, if the community makes an individual feel he or she belongs to it, it can positively influence him or her.

Note

1. From Abramson, A., & Malnic, E. (1991, August). Wounded girl begs for mercy—but is slain. *Los Angeles Times*, pp. B1, B4. Used with permission.

References

Abrahamson, A., & Malnic, E. (1991, August). Wounded girl begs for mercy—but is slain. *Los Angeles Times*, pp. B1, B4.
The California Council on Criminal Justice. State Task Force on Gangs and Drugs (1989). *Report to the Governor of California, The Honorable George Deukmejian*. Sacramento: The Task Force.
California Senate Committee on Children and Youth. (1975, November 14). Meeting on Juvenile Gang Warfare (Minutes).
Cloward, R. A., & Ohlin, L. E. (1960). Delinquency and opportunity: A theory of delinquent gangs. New York: Free Press.
Cowen, S., & Lang, L. (1991). Application of the principles of community-based programs. *Journal of the U. S. Public Health Service, 106*, 269-270.
Cohen, A. K. (1955). *Delinquent boys: The culture of the gang*. Glencoe, IL: Free Press.
Donovan, J. (1988). *An introduction to street gangs in California*. Report for Senator John Garamendi, 5th Senate District. Sacramento: California State Legislature.
Downes, C. M. (1966). *The delinquent solution*. London: Routledge & Kegan Paul.
Fox, J. R. (1985). Mission impossible? Social work practice with black urban youth gangs. *Social Work, 30*, 25-31.
Gates, D. F. (1990, November). Gang violence in Los Angeles. *The Police Chief*, pp. 20-22.
Hagedorn, J. M. (1988). *People and folks: Gangs, crime and the underclass in a rustbelt city*. Chicago: Lake View Press.
Hawkins, J. D., & Weis, J. G. (1985). The social development model: An integrated approach to delinquency prevention. *Journal of Primary Prevention, 6*, 73-97.
Holguin, R. (1991, August 6). Head of anti-gang unit denies operating police "snitch network." *Los Angeles Times*, p. B11.
Horowitz, R. (1987). Community tolerance of gang violence. *Social Problems, 34*, 437-450.
Huff, C. R. (1989). Youth gangs and public policy. *Crime and Delinquency, 35*, 524-537.
Klein, M. W. (1969). Gang cohesiveness, delinquency and a street-work program. *Journal of Research in Crime and Delinquency, 6*, 135-166.

104   Impact of Gang Violence

Kornhauser, R. R. (1978). *Social sources of delinquency.* Chicago: University of Chicago Press.

Lacayo, R. (1991, April 1). Back to the beat. *Time,* pp. 22-24.

McBride, W. D., & Jackson, R. K. (1989, June). In Los Angeles County, a high-tech assist in the war on gangs. *The Police Chief,* pp. 28-31.

Miller, W. B. (1981). *Crime by youth gangs and groups in the United States.* National Institute for Juvenile Justice and Delinquency Prevention. Washington, DC: U. S. Department of Justice.

Morash, M. (1983). Gangs, groups, and delinquency. *The British Journal of Criminology, 23,* 309-331.

Patterson, G. R., DeBaryshe, B. D., & Ramsey, E. (1989). A developmental perspective on antisocial behavior. Special issue: Children and their development: Knowledge base, research agenda, and social policy application. *American Psychologist, 44,* 329-335.

Pierce, D., & Ramsay, T. G. (1990, November). Gang violence: Not just a big city problem. *The Police Chief,* pp. 24-25.

Prothrow-Stith, D. (1991). Boston's violence prevention project. *Journal of the U.S. Public Health Service, 106,* 237-238.

Roper, W. L. (1991). Opening keynote address: The prevention of minority youth violence must begin despite risks and imperfect understanding. *Journal of the U.S. Public Health Service, 106,* 229-231.

Seidman, E. (1986). Justice, values, and social science: Unexamined premises. In E. Seidman & J. Rappaport (Eds.), *Redefining social problems* (pp. 235-258). New York: Plenum.

Sessions, W. S. (1990, November). Gang violence and organized crime. *The Police Chief,* p. 17.

Shannon, T. R. (1983). *Urban problems in sociological perspective.* Illinois: Wareland Press.

Sheerer, M. (1985). Effects of group intervention on moral development of distressed youth in Israel. *Journal of Youth and Adolescence, 14,* 513-527.

Spergel, I. A. (1984). Violent gangs in Chicago: In search of social policy. *Social Service Review, 60,* 94-131.

Suttles, G. P. (1968). *The social order of the slum.* Chicago: University of Chicago Press.

Thompson, D. W., & Jason, L. A. (1988). Street gangs and preventive interventions. *Criminal Justice and Behavior, 15,* 323-333.

Tolan, P. (1988). Socio-economic, family, and social stress correlates of adolescent antisocial and delinquent behavior. *Journal of Abnormal Child Psychology, 16,* 317-331.

Wilson, W. F. (1987). *The truly disadvantaged.* Chicago: University of Chicago Press.

Wilson-Brewer, R., & Jacklin, B. (1991). Violence prevention strategies targeted at the general population of minority youth. *Journal of the U.S. Public Health Service, 106,* 270-271.

7

A Clinical Model for the Prevention of Gang Violence and Homicide¹

ARMANDO MORALES

The Gang Problem

A gang may be defined as a peer group of persons in a lower-, middle-, or upper-class community who participate in activities that are either harmful to themselves and/or others in society (Morales, 1978). Urban gangs are a growing health and mental health crisis; their antisocial behavior is resulting in thousands of homicides and assaults each year and their involvement with drugs, both as consumers and as dealers, is causing untold human destruction in central city communities, particularly among poor families. Gangs have been with us since the beginning of civilization, but the concept of gangs was first reported in the literature by a former gang member, St. Augustine (A.D. 354-430), more than 1,600 years ago (St. Augustine, 1949). His father was described as a womanizer, drinker, and gambler; and his mother, whom he loved dearly, was a pious Christian who had difficulty controlling St. Augustine during his adolescent years. In his book *Confessions*, he demonstrates an acute understanding of the psychology of adolescent gangs with his discovery that committing a crime in the company of others further enhances the gratifications derived from it.

The first youth gangs in the United States were seen in Philadelphia in the 1840s. They were known to be very violent (Davis & Haller, 1973). During the pre-Civil War period, intense conflict was also seen in New York among white adolescent and young adult gangs attempting to establish control over a particular neighborhood or "turf" (Asbury, 1927). When these gangs fought, police were reluctant to intervene during these 2- and 3-day gang wars. Such intense, prolonged violent conflict is not seen today among gangs. Rather, drive-by shootings, characteristic of the 1920s Capone era, are the more common expression of violence between gangs.

Thrasher (1963), in his classic 1920s studies of youth gangs in Chicago, discovered 1,313 gangs in that city alone, comprised mostly of non-minority "Whites." This represented approximately 65 gangs per 100,000 persons in the general population, a far greater ratio than Los Angeles's 100,000 gang members in 900 gangs in 1990, representing 11 gangs per 100,000 persons in the general population (Morales & Sheafor, 1992).

There are at least five common theories explaining the underlying causes of gangs, as follows. The first is that the gang is a natural progression from, and the consequence of, a youth's search for excitement in a frustrating and limiting environment, usually the result of a general breakdown of social controls, and characterized by persons with few social ties—such as immigrants (Thrasher, 1963).

A second theory is that gang members were reared in female-dominated households and consequently, in adolescence, the gang "provided the first real opportunity to learn essential aspects of the male role in the context of peers facing similar problems of sex role identification" (Miller, 1958).

A third perspective sees the gang as the collective solution of young, lower-class males placed in a situation of stress, where opportunities for the attainment of wealth and/or status through legitimate channels are blocked. In response, the gang develops a subculture or "contra-culture" (Cloward & Ohlin, 1960; Cohen, 1955).

A fourth theory challenges the above "blocked out" subculture theory, stating that it explains too much delinquency. Rather, gangs are seen to exist because adolescents are in a state of suspension between childhood and adulthood; hence, they spend most of their time with peers and are anxious about both their identity as males and their acceptance by the peer group (gang). They conform to the norms of the gang because not to do so would threaten their status (Matza, 1964).

A fifth theoretical causal factor involves the family. In a study of East Los Angeles Latino gang and non-gang juvenile probation camp graduates, I found that gang members, significantly more often that non-gang members, came from families exhibiting more family breakdown, greater poverty, poorer housing; more alcoholism, drug addiction, and major chronic illness; and more family members involved with law enforcement and correctional agencies (Morales, 1963). In the face of these overwhelming problems, the youngster turns to the gang as a *surrogate family*. This observation was again confirmed in subsequent work with gangs (Morales, 1978, 1982; Morales & Sheafor, 1989, 1992). Vigil arrived at a similar conclusion and also saw the gang as a surrogate family (Vigil, 1988). In the gang surrogate family, the gang member receives affection, understanding, recognition, loyalty, and emotional and physical protection. In this respect the gang is psychologically adaptive rather than maladaptive. The challenge for the health and mental health professions, therefore, is to either stop or prevent the cycle of violence in youths who persist in associating with dangerous gangs in the pursuit of meeting their needs for status, self-esteem, and affection at the expense of serious injury or even their lives. Prevention theories and concepts applied to gang member victims and their respective families may hold promise for the health and mental health professions in addressing this major social concern.

Primary prevention in a public health context involves averting the initial occurrence of a disease, defect, or injury. Primary prevention in homicide requires national efforts to be directed at social, cultural, educational, technological, and legal aspects of the macro environment, which facilitate the perpetuation of the United States' extremely high homicide rate—indeed, a tall order. A national strategy would involve public education about the seriousness of ramifications of violence, contributing factors, high-risk groups, and the need for social policy as a physical health and mental health priority in the United States. The topic must become a higher priority in medical schools and schools of nursing, social work, and psychology. At the community level self-help groups, social planning councils, and other civic groups need to work toward educating U.S. citizens about the causal relationship of alcohol, illegal drugs, firearms, and television violence to homicide and violence (USDHHS, 1986). In theory these strategies, when directed at high-risk populations, are supposed to reduce those conditions that are seen as contributing to violence and homicide.

Secondary prevention in a public health context concerns the cessation or slowing down of a health problem's progression. It involves the early detection and case finding by which more serious morbidity may be decreased. In application of this concept to homicide, such case finding requires the identification of persons showing early signs of behavioral and social problems that are related to increased risk for subsequent homicide victimization. Variables such as family violence, childhood and adolescent aggression, school violence, truancy and dropping out of school, and substance abuse are early indicators of many persons who later become perpetrators of violence and homicide. Secondary prevention and intervention strategies with individuals already exhibiting these early symptoms interrupt a pattern that would have later resulted in serious violence or homicide (USDHHS, 1986, pp. 46-50).

Tertiary prevention pertains to those situations in which a health problem is already well established, but efforts can still be made to prevent further progress toward disability and death. In the case of homicide the problems of greatest concern are those of interpersonal conflict and nonfatal violence, which appear to have a high risk for homicide. Aggravated assault is one early significant predictor related to homicide (USDHHS, 1986, p. 50). In a study in Kansas, in 25% of the homicides either the victim or the perpetrator had previously been arrested for an assault or a disturbance (Police Foundation). Victims of aggravated assault such as spouses or gang members are especially a high risk for becoming homicide cases.

Attempts have been made in developing program models aimed at preventing youth violence and homicide—although some of these programs are not specifically aimed at *gang* homicide prevention. These educational, court, and community-based programs seem to be functioning mainly at the primary (reducing conditions contributing to homicide) and secondary (identifying persons showing early signs of sociobehavioral problems) prevention levels. A few of these programs as examples of prevention models will be discussed.

Educational Prevention Models

The *Boston Youth Program* instituted in four Boston high schools had a curriculum on anger and violence. The 10-session curriculum provided: (a) information on adolescent violence and homicide; (b) the discussion of anger as a normal, potentially constructive emotion; (c) knowledge in developing alternatives to fighting; (d) role playing and videotapes; and (e) the fostering of nonviolent values. Following the completion of the program, an evaluation of a control group (no curriculum) and an experimental group (curriculum) revealed that there was a significant positive change of attitude in the experimental group. The researchers cautioned, however, that further study had to delineate the actual impact the curriculum will have on actual *behavior* and the longevity of the impact (USDHHS, 1986, pp. 235-236). The Boston Youth Program was directed at minority students, but it was not indicated whether any of these students were gang members.

Another school-based prevention program functioning in the City of Paramount in Los Angeles County is called the *Paramount Plan*. This was designed to be a "gang prevention" model and, unlike the Boston Youth Program and Peer Dynamics, which target high school youths, it is an educational model directed at all elementary school fifth and sixth graders in the school district. The program consists of neighborhood parent meetings and an anti-gang curriculum taught to students in school for 15 weeks. Prior to the program 50% of students were "undecided" about joining gangs. After the 15 weeks, 90% said they would not join gangs (Ostos, 1987).

No mention was made about the 10% of students who did not change their minds about joining gangs. In poor urban areas where there are gangs, it is only about 5% of youths who become delinquents and/or join gangs. In other words, at least 95% of youths do not join gangs, even without a gang prevention program such as the Paramount Plan. Further research is needed to determine if those in the 10% who did *not* change their minds about joining gangs actually do so and second, whether they later become either perpetrators or victims of gang homicide. Perhaps one of the major research challenges is to be able to measure *what* was prevented.

Court and Community-Based Programs

In Baltimore, Maryland, *Strike II* was developed as a court-based program linking juvenile justice with health care. Its clients were court adjudicated first-time offenders (secondary prevention) for violent crimes, assault, robbery, arson, and breaking and entering. Noninstitutionalized probationers were eligible for the program, which was a probation requirement. This multidiscipline program employed paralegal staff, counselors, social workers, and psychiatrists. The juvenile probationers were involved in five programs: recreation, education, job readiness, ongoing counseling, and medical care as needed. These services were in addition to traditional probation supervision.

The recidivism rate for Strike II clients was only 7%, compared to 35% statewide and 65% for those leaving corrections institutions. The basic cost (excluding medical and job readiness services) was $100 per client (Johns Hopkins Hospital). The Strike II program dealt in large part with violent juveniles with a physical health/mental health, educational, employment, juvenile justice program with resulting impressive results. Although gang members were not mentioned specifically, it would appear that with a reduction in recidivism, that is, becoming less violent, these perpetrators would have also been at reduced risk for becoming violence/homicide victims.

In 1978 the state California Youth Authority (CYA) reported its findings concerning its *Gang Violence Reduction Project* in East Los Angeles. The project's basic strategy was to (a) promote peace among gangs through negotiation and (b) provide positive activities for gang members. Directors maintain they reduced gang homicides in East Los Angeles by 55%: from 11 homicides in 7 months one year, down to 5 homicides during a similar 7-month period the following year. The project researchers admitted that "any judgment that a relationship exists between the changes in a gang related homicide and violent incident statistics and the activities of the Gang Violence Reduction Project must be based on inference" (CYA, 1978).

Another community-based peace treaty program aimed at high-risk gang youths, patterned after the 1969 "Philadelphia Plan," is the *Community Youth Gang Services Corporation* (CYGS) in Los Angeles. CYGS counselors in 14 street teams were able to convince 44 of 200 gangs they worked with to come to the table to develop a peace treaty. During the period the peace agreement was in effect, from Thanksgiving of 1986 though the New Year's holiday of 1987, there was only *one* act of violence among the 44 gangs. The peace treaties model can buy time for all concerned, but if society does not respond with the needed resources (jobs, training, physical health/mental health services, education), peace treaties are very difficult to maintain. Obviously, all the above approaches are needed.

Continuing efforts have to be made in further refining homicide prevention models for them to correspond more closely with the specific type of homicide one wishes to prevent. There are different types of homicide that vary according to circumstances. Robbery, spousal, and gang homicide are all different and require different prevention strategies. If, for example, Asians are at extremely high risk for being robbed and murdered at 2 a.m. in "Uptown, U.S.A.," through a community education effort, Asians would be informed about the high homicide risk in visiting "Uptown" at 2 a.m. Adhering to the warning could immediately reduce the number of Asian homicide victims.

In addition to attempting to get a "close fit" between the prevention model and the specific type of homicide, it is equally important that the high-risk person be clearly identified in order to maximize the impact of the prevention model. In the educational and community-based violence prevention models previously discussed, the focus of intervention appeared to be more on the perpetrator or the "pre-perpetrator" (the person showing early behavioral signs indicating that he or she might become a perpetrator) who was at high risk for committing a violent act. In theory all potential victims in an *unspecified* population are spared victimization when the perpetrator ceases to be violent. Furthermore, there did not seem to be specific prevention programmatic strategies focusing on the violence *victim* or the person most likely to become a victim. What seems to be needed is a guideline or framework that assists in the identification of high-risk gang members.

When California is used as an example, Table 7.1 represents a "general to specific" profile framework for identifying and zeroing in on the high-risk gang members who will be the target population for homicide prevention.

I developed a hospital- and community-based youth gang psychosocial homicide prevention model in which social workers or other mental health practitioners play a key intervention role. The focus of this prevention model will be on the gang members who actually become violence or homicide victims of a gang and are taken to the hospital. In Table 7.1 these victims would be gang members found in items 2b and 2c. In this respect the prevention model is largely tertiary in nature. However, it becomes a primary prevention model when intervention strategies are aimed at younger children and latency age siblings of the victims who are not yet gang members. By preventing children in high-risk families from becoming future gang members, it may significantly reduce the likelihood of the children being killed since gang members are 60 times more likely to be killed than persons in the general population (600/100,000 versus 10/100,000).

Health professionals in community clinics and hospitals are actually "in the trenches," dealing with thousands of violence and homicide casualties related to gang violence. These professionals are usually the first to touch these bodies and, in medical settings, they function in a tertiary prevention role, literally trying to control the bleeding and save

Table 7.1 Area and Demographic Characteristics Related to Homicide Risk

I. United States	(one of the most violent countries in the world, ranked #5 out of 41 countries).[a]
II. California	(along with Southern states, ranks among the most violent states)[b]
III. Los Angeles	(among the more violent cities in the United States)[c]
IV. Inner City (L.A.)	(the poorest areas, often the scene of most violent crime)
A. Minority Groups	(overrepresented among the disadvantaged and poor, and those residing in the inner city)
1. Profile of Perpetrators and Victims	
a. Males	(4 to 5 times more likely than females to be killed)
b. Age	(15 to 25 age category at highest risk)
c. Substance Abuse	(found in 50% to 66% of cases)
d. Low Education	(50% school drop-out rate not uncommon)
e. Low Income	(high unemployment, many living in poverty)
2. Gangs	(quite prevalent in inner city and a product of social disorganization, classism, and racism)[d]
a. Minor Assaults	(gang members are at high risk for being assaulted)
b. Aggravated Assaults	(gang members are at high risk for being victims of aggravated assault; usually occurs 20 to 35 times more often than homicide)
c. Homicide	(gang members are at high risk for becoming homicide victims, rate being 600 per 100,000 in the 50,000 gang member population)[e]

a. Mark L. Rosenberg and James A. Mercy, "Homicide: Epidemiologic Analysis at the National Level," in *Bulletin of the New York Academy of Medicine*, Vol. 62, No. 5, June 1986, p. 382.
b. Mark L. Rosenberg, p. 390.
c. Harold M. Rose, "Can We Substantially Lower Homicide Risk in the Nation's Larger Black Communities?" in *Report of the Secretary's Task force*, p. 191.
d. Irving A. Spergel, "Violent Gangs in Chicago: In Search of Social Policy," *Social Service Review*, Vol. 58, No. 2, June 1984, pp. 201-202.
e. Armando Morales, "Hispanic Gang Violence and Homicide." (Paper commissioned by the Research Conference on Violence and Homicide in Hispanic Communities, sponsored by the Office of Minority Health, Department of Health and Human Services, the National Institute of Mental Health, and the U.S. Centers for Disease Control, University of California, Los Angeles, September 14-15, 1987, p. 13.)

lives. Wounded gang victims of gang violence are in reality a captive audience, which creates an excellent intervention opportunity for secondary prevention.

By the physician, social worker, nurse, or other health practitioners on the hospital emergency room team inquiring about *how* the victim was injured, which may also be confirmed by police, family members, or interested parties, professionals could ascertain if the violence was "gang related." Through staff in-service training concerning gangs and their culture, health staff would be able to determine whether the victim was a gang member. Specifically, gang dress codes, mannerisms, graffiti, language, tattoos, and other gang symbols could either help establish or rule out the gang identity of the victim. Police, family members, peers, and/or witnesses could also be good sources for gang identity confirmation.

If the injuries were caused by gang members and the victim is a gang member, a designated health team member (the social worker, psychologist, or psychiatrist) would be responsible for referring the matter to the hospital's "SCAN Team." SCAN Team refers to Suspected Child Abuse and Neglect, or in some hospitals it refers to Supporting Child Adult Network (Tatara, Morgan, & Portner, 1986). SCAN Teams, which are found in many hospitals, are composed of multidisciplinary health staff in which at least one member is a social worker. SCAN Teams were originally developed to investigate suspected child sexual or physical abuse or neglect cases coming to the team's attention in medical settings. In cases of suspected child abuse and for the protection of the child, SCAN Teams are required to take immediate action by involving law enforcement and the child welfare department.

Our gang homicide prevention model would require that gang violence victims also become a SCAN Team intervention priority. However, one additional social worker or mental health practitioner on the SCAN Team would be a gang "specialist" and would have primary treatment coordinating responsibility with the gang victim, his or her family, and the community.

Although not intended, the emergency room provides access to a high-risk population (victims and families) that often is too embarrassed, frightened, or reluctant to seek assistance from traditional mental health agencies that make the anonymity of large, busy, impersonal hospital less threatening (USDHHS, 1986, p. 246). Additionally, medical crises may make some persons psychologically vulnerable, hence, more amenable to change during the crisis period.

In working with gang members who have been seriously injured as a result of gang assault, I have found that often this is when their psychological defenses are down as they are suffering adjustment disorder or posttraumatic stress disorder symptoms (PTSD). In the acute stage of PTSD symptoms, victims may have recurrent, intrusive, distressing recollections of the event, including nightmares, flashbacks, intense stress at exposure to events resembling the traumatic event, persistent avoidance of stimuli associated with the event, sleeping problems, hypervigilance, anxiety, and fear. They are sometimes reluctant to leave the home and even become fearful of their own friends in gang "uniform."

During this acute stage, which may last about 6 months, they are quite motivated to abandon gangbanging (gang fighting). If the social worker or other mental health practitioner is not the primary therapist, arrangements should be made for the youngster to receive prompt treatment for PTSD regardless of whether he or she is hospitalized, because untreated PTSD may become chronic and last for years. It is at this point that the mental health practitioner can also obtain needed employment, educational, recreational, or training resources for the vulnerable gang member. The parents may also be emotionally vulnerable, having just gone through an experience in which they almost lost their child. They may be more willing to accept services for themselves if needed, and/or for younger siblings who might be showing some early behavioral signs of problems (deteriorating school performance, truancy, aggressiveness). Helping the family and young siblings is a primary prevention role because these efforts may result in preventing future gang members (perpetrators or victims) from developing in this at-risk family.

There may also be situations in which the wounded gang member arrives deceased at the hospital or dies during or after surgery. This case would still be referred to the SCAN Team social worker for service. The focus of help would be—with the family's permission—in helping the parents and siblings deal with grief and in providing other assistance they might need in burying their loved one. If there are adolescent gang members in the family, they may be quite angry and want to retaliate and "get even" for their brother's or sister's death. If not already involved, the social worker would call upon community gang group agencies to assist in reducing further conflict. If there are younger siblings in the family, an assessment would be made of their needs and efforts made to mobilize resources to meet those needs. These intervention strategies would have the objective of preventing future homicides in a high-risk family.

The preceding gang homicide prevention model, operating from a medical-based agency, is presented to illustrate how mental health

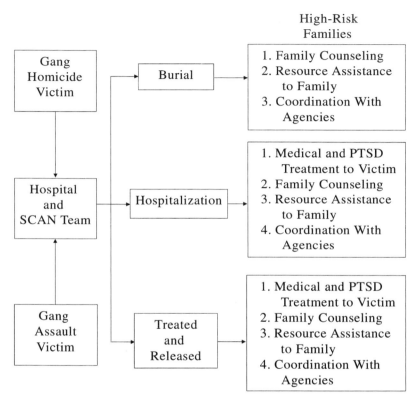

Figure 7.1. Gang Homicide Psychosocial Prevention Model*

*This gang homicide psychosocial prevention model and Table 7.1 was originally developed by Armando Morales and presented in a paper commissioned by the Research Conference on Violence and Homicide in Hispanic Communities, sponsored by the Office of Minority Health, Department of Health and Human Services, the National Institutes of Mental Health, and the U.S. Centers for Disease Control, University of California, Los Angeles, September 14-15, 1987, p. 19).

practitioners may be able to have intervention impact on a very serious problem shortening the life of many poor, inner-city youths. Other models can be developed. Figure 7.1 demonstrates the various intervention strategies.

Conclusion

Urban gang violence and homicide are spreading throughout the nation. In the most affected areas, such as Los Angeles County with 100,000 gang members and between 600 and 700 gang-related homicides a year, law enforcement agencies are now acknowledging that their social control methods (arrests and incarceration) are not working. Politicians' "get tough and build more juvenile and adult correctional facilities" rhetoric is becoming more difficult to sell to the taxpayers in periods of economic recession.

Our health and mental health practitioners have not necessarily flocked to help the inner-city with its alarming homicide rates, impacted significantly by gang-related violence and homicide. Gang members are feared, and our countertransference stance makes us avoid them, fueled in part by a fatalistic attitude about our ability to prevent violence and homicide. Such attitudes are usually more like those of poor, underdeveloped countries toward infectious diseases which, due to the lack of resources and/or knowledge, cause apathy.

Health professionals cannot hide from the gang violence problem as the wounded and the dead keep piling up in emergency rooms and morgues. This chapter discussed a unique opportunity to stop the violence cycle by focusing intervention efforts on the family members (particularly younger siblings) of the deceased or seriously wounded gang members, utilizing the "Gang Homicide Psychosocial Prevention Model." Such an approach would be primary prevention intervention, and hospitals could play a significant role in reducing gang violence and homicide. Furthermore, if mental health practitioners in private practice could incorporate the legal *pro bono* concept into their work (providing free service to clients as a public service), and "adopt" one affected bereaved family, the cycle might be stopped for those families.

Note

1. This paper was presented at the National Conference on Substance Abuse and Gang Violence, March 30, 1990, Los Angeles, California. A more detailed version of this work appeared in Armando Morales and Bradford W. Sheafor, *Social Work: A Profession of Many Faces, Fifth Edition* (Boston: Allyn and Bacon, 1989), pp. 605-630.

References

Asbury, H. (1927). *The gangs of New York: An informational history of the underworld.* New York: Knopf.

Augustine, Saint. (1949). *Confessions.* New York: Modern Library.

Boston Youth Program, The. (1986). In USDHHS, *Report of the secretary's task force* (pp. 235-236). Washington, DC: Government Printing Office.

California Youth Authority (CYA). (1978, November). *Gang violence reduction project second evaluation report: October 1977–May 1978.*

California Youth Authority (CYA). (1985). *Early gang intervention.* Proceeds of Transfer of Knowledge Workshop, California Youth Authority, Office of Criminal Justice Planning.

Cloward, R. A., & Ohlin, L. E. (1960). *Delinquency and opportunity.* New York: Free Press.

Cohen, A. K. (1955). *Delinquent boys: The culture of the gang.* Glencoe, IL: Free Press.

Davis, A., & Haller, M. (Eds.). (1973). *The people of Philadelphia.* Philadelphia: Temple University Press.

Johns Hopkins Hospital. *Strike II, Hopkins adolescent program.* Baltimore, MD: Author.

Matza, D. (1964). *Delinquency and Drift.* New York: John Wiley.

Miller, W. B. (1958). Lower class culture as a generating milieu of gang delinquency. *Journal of Social Issues, 14,* 15-19.

Morales, A. (1963). *A study of recidivism of Mexican-American junior forestry camp graduates.* Unpublished master's thesis, School of Social Work, University of Southern California.

Morales, A. (1978). The need for nontraditional mental health programs in the barrio. In J. M. Casas & S. E. Keefe (Eds.), *Family and mental health in the Mexican-American community* (Monograph No. 7, p. 133). Los Angeles: UCLA Spanish-Speaking Mental Health Research Center.

Morales, A. (1982). The Mexican American gang member: Evaluation an treatment. In R. M. Becerra, M. Karno, & J. Escobar (Eds.), *Mental health and Hispanic Americans: Clinical perspectives.* New York: Grune & Stratton.

Morales, A. (1987, September 14-15). *Hispanic gang violence and homicide.* Paper commissioned by the Research Conference on Violence and Homicide in Hispanic Communities, University of California, Los Angeles.

Morales, A., & Sheafor, B. W. (1989). *Social work: A profession of many faces* (5th ed.). Boston: Allyn & Bacon.

Morales, A., & Sheafor, B. W. (1992). *Social work: A profession of many faces* (6th ed.). Boston: Allyn & Bacon.

Ostos, T. (1987). *Alternatives to gang membership.* Unpublished paper, Paramount School District, Los Angeles County, California.

Police Foundation. *Domestic violence and the police: Studies in Detroit and Kansas City.* Washington, DC: The Foundation.

Rose, H. M. (1986). Can we substantially lower homicide risk in the nation's larger black communities? In USDHHS, *Report of the secretary's task force* (p. 191). Washington, DC: Government Printing Office.

Rosenberg, M. L., & Mercy, J. A. (1986, June). Homicide: Epidemiologic analysis at the national level. *Bulletin of the New York Academy of Medicine, 62*(5), 382, 390.

Spergel, I. A. (1984, June). Violent gangs in Chicago: In search of social policy. *Social Service Review, 58*(2), 201-202.

Tatara, T., Morgan, H., & Portner. (1986, November-December). SCAN: Providing preventive services in an urban setting. *Children Today*, pp. 17-22.

Thrasher, F. M. (1963). *The gang: A study of 1313 gangs in Chicago.* Chicago: University of Chicago Press.

U.S. Department of Health and Human Services (USDHHS). (1986, January). *Report of the secretary's task force on black and minority health* (Vol. 5). Washington, DC: Government Printing Office.

Vigil, J. D. (1988). *Barrio gangs.* Austin: University of Texas Press.

PART IV

Survivors of Gang Violence

8

Psychological Effects of Exposure to Gang Violence

TIA ALANE NISHIMOTO HOFFER
RICHARD C. CERVANTES

In the United States, gangs have had a long and notorious history and have grown and developed into a large subculture. *Gang* is a term delineating a "peer group of persons in a lower-, middle-, or upper-class community who participate in activities that are either harmful to themselves and/or others in society" (Morales, 1987), and who "interact at a high rate among themselves to the exclusion of other groups, have a group name, claim a neighborhood or other territory, and engage in criminal and other anti-social behavior on a regular basis" (California Council on Criminal Justice, 1986). The literature on delinquency and gangs is very extensive and spans 70 years. Studies have often examined the sociological, psychological, economical, and political issues influencing gangs. It is important to review some of these areas of research on gang members and other delinquent adolescents in order to understand the complexity of the phenomenon.

In terms of the sociological factors influencing gangs, Vigil (1990) concluded that gang members gain status, identification, a sense of belonging, and protection through their gang involvement (Collins, 1979; Vigil, 1990). Families that are economically deprived and struggling may be another factor leading youths to turn to gangs as a source of both emotional and economic support (Abrahamsen, 1960; Adler, Ovando, & Hocevar, 1984; Andry, 1960; Daum & Bieliauskas, 1983;

Glueck & Glueck, 1968), but research contradicting this assertion has been presented by Bowker and Klein (1983).

The literature has also examined various psychological factors common among gang members (Bustamante, Thomas, & James, 1990; Cartwright, Tomson, & Schwartz, 1975; Klein, 1971; Krisberg, 1974; Yablonsky, 1962). Bustamante, Thomas, and James concluded that the intellectual capabilities of the gang members studied were average to above average, with no signs of neurological impairments. The degree of anxiety, anger, insecurity, guilt, dysphoria, fear, and affective sensitivity varied among the gang members assessed. The only consistent factor among all participants of the study was the feelings of mistrust toward other people.

Although most of the studies have examined the gang phenomenon from the perspective of social and psychological influences on gang involvement, they have generally not addressed the psychological effects that violence has on the gang members. Within the gang value system, violence varies in frequency, intensity, and type. Moore (1990) found that gangs in California have become more violent due to the availability of high-powered weaponry. This increase in violence within the gang increases the potential exposure gang members may have to violence. Gang members are often exposed to and vulnerable to attacks and other forms of violent victimization (Singer, 1981). Violent behavior has been seen by some as a response to victimization. Singer stated that 94% of gang members who had been victims of violence also disclosed that they had committed a serious assault at some point during their gang involvement. Alcohol and other drugs have also contributed to the escalation of aggression and violence among gangs. In 1979 the Department of Justice surveyed California state prison inmates and found that 2 out of 5 were under the influence of alcohol or drugs either near or at the time their offense was committed. More recent national data suggest that the connection between violent crime and substance abuse has in fact become stronger (U.S. Department of Justice, 1988).

Since there have not been any investigations of the effects of this increasing violence on gang youths, it is important to understand how these youths manifest trauma and stress related to frequent exposure to violence. This information is important in serving as a basis for more effective therapeutic work with youths who are both involved in and exposed to violent gang activity. While several studies have examined the various psychological precursors to gang membership, there have been no studies published that examine the psychological sequelae of constant exposure to gang-like violent events.

Posttraumatic Stress and Exposure to Violence

Posttraumatic Stress Disorder (PTSD) occurs following a person's exposure to severe stress or trauma that is outside the realm of normal experience (APA, 1987). It is a universal disorder that crosses the boundaries of ethnicity, age, sex, class, and culture (Helzer, Robins, & McEvoy, 1987). PTSD ranges from mild to severe and can be acute or delayed. Delayed onset of PTSD occurs at least six months after the traumatic event (APA, 1987). As the severity and quantity of the stressor increases, there is a corresponding increase in the severity of the symptoms of PTSD (Grinker & Spiegel, 1945). Symptoms such as sleep disturbances, intrusive thoughts, hypervigilance, and emotionality are commonly observed among people suffering from PTSD.

Posttraumatic Stress Disorder (PTSD) has been experienced most commonly by individuals who have been subjected to the trauma of war. Recent research on PTSD has been conducted most extensively with Vietnam veterans. Other research has been conducted to investigate the occurrence of PTSD among children and adolescents subjected to natural disasters, rape trauma, and violence, and also among political refugees (see, for example, Cervantes, Salgado de Snyder, & Padilla, 1989).

Given the increasing level of violence that gang members experience, one can argue that this experience is analogous to the combat situation that Vietnam veterans experienced. The clinical diagnosis of Posttraumatic Stress Disorder has been investigated and found to be a useful and relevant diagnosis of the experience of Vietnam veterans and others who have experienced traumas. Both Vietnam veterans and gang members have similar experiences in terms of being both the victims and the perpetrators of violence. There are many other similarities that can be drawn between the experience of Vietnam veterans and gang members: stress from an unfamiliar and hostile environment, alienation, lack of social support, survivor guilt, alcohol and other drug use, sensation-seeking behavior, and lack of trust (Catherall, 1986; Daum & Bieliauskas, 1983; Hall & Hall, 1987; Lucking, 1986; Martinez, Hays, & Solway, 1979; Solkoff, Gray, & Keill, 1986; Stonequist, 1937; Wilson & Zigelbaum,

1985). Therefore, the investigation of Posttraumatic Stress Disorder in conjunction with the urban street violence that gang members experience seemed to be a logical step in gaining essential insight into the treatment and rehabilitation of gang members.

This study focused on Latino gang members in the greater Los Angeles area. "Barrio" (turf) gangs composed of Latino members have existed in the Los Angeles area for 40 to 50 years. They have grown and solidified their values and beliefs to assert their identity in an often economically depriving and oppressive society. A small percentage of Latino youths in the United States are involved in the gang subculture; estimates range from 4% to 10% (Morales, 1982). Though their numbers are small, it is important to understand the psychology of this population as our communities come to be increasingly affected, both directly and indirectly, by the criminal and violent activities of these youths.

Wilson (1988) states that those who are exposed to and involved in the "grotesque realities of killing and destruction" often suffer from a traumatic and lasting impact on their sense of self. Helzer, Robins, and McEvoy (1987) noted that PTSD can be found in the general population through epidemiologic studies, but is more prevalent among people who have been either exposed to or subjected to physical violence (3.5%). The violence that gang members are exposed to leaves them vulnerable to become not only victims but also perpetrators of the violence (Singer, 1981). Exposure to violence among many gang members is multifaceted: being "jumped in" or "jumped out" of the gang; fighting members of either your gang or a rival gang with fists, knives, or guns; drive-by shootings; being beaten up or stabbed; seeing your homeboy or homegirl being beaten up, stabbed, or killed. Rocha-Perez (1989) connected Posttraumatic Stress Disorder with gang violence. She views the violence as a trauma—not just a criminal problem necessitating punishment, but one that requires treatment as well. The effects of victimization should not be taken less seriously though the society may have tolerance for crimes committed against victim-offenders who have a prior relationship.

It appears from the literature that the experience of combat in a war situation or through violent gang activities may increase the violent behavior of an individual. Combat veterans have been found to be significantly more violent then either the noncombat veterans or nonveterans (Boulanger & Kadushin, 1986). Horowitz and Solomon (1978) stated that it is difficult for some violent veterans to control impulses when real violence occurs; when human beings are dehumanized or devalued; and when reality and fantasy images are confused. Among gang members it is possible that the exposure to violence and the expression of PTSD symptoms through flashbacks may contribute to their further involvement in violence.

Methods

Subjects

Subjects for the study were male Latino and Chicano gang members, between the ages of 14 and 18, who were incarcerated at the Probation Department of Los Angeles County. Eighty subjects were included in the study and were assessed on their level of identification in the gang. Subjects who qualified to participate in the study are as follows: active gang members, gang members who are beginning to leave the gang and the gang life-style, and former gang members who are no long a part of the gang or the gang life-style.

Each subject was asked to complete the written questionnaires: the demographic questionnaire; the Gang Identification Scale; the Brief Symptom Inventory; the California High School Substance Abuse Survey; the Mississippi Scale for Combat Related PTSD; the Social Support Index; the Traumatic Violence Scale. The demographic questionnaire obtained information concerning the subjects' age, sex, SES, education, and extent of drug use. The Gang Identification Scale assessed the subjective level of gang identification of the subjects. The Traumatic Violence Scale might have potentially created some stress as a result of the item contents, so it was administered last. Subjects were administered the questionnaires within the classrooms of the Los Angeles Probation Camps, Camp Karl Holton and Camp Routh. A teacher was present for each class. Three separate research assistants administered the questionnaires and answered all questions from the participants.

Instruments

The following six self-report questionnaires were administered in group settings. The first instrument was the demographic questionnaire that incorporated questions designed for this study, along with questions gathered from Mancillas (1986) in order to gather the necessary information specific to gang membership. The second instrument, the Brief Symptom Inventory (BSI) (Derogatis, 1975), was used to assess the participant's psychological state at the time of testing. The third instrument was the California High School Substance Abuse Survey (Skager, Fisher, & Maddahian, 1986). The fourth instrument was the Mississippi Scale for Combat Related PTSD (Keane, Caddell, & Taylor, 1988). The fifth instrument was the Social Support Index (McCubbin, Patterson, & Glynn, 1982), used to assess the degree of social support through self-report measures. The sixth instrument was the Traumatic Violence Severity Scale, which was used to assess the degree of traumatic violence exposure of gangs (TVS) (Gallers, 1984). Some wording changes were made on the various instruments in order to measure specific gang violence experiences. For more extensive information regarding instrumentation, see Hoffer (1991).

Appropriateness of Instruments for Study Sample

Prior to conducting formal data analyses, a series of reliability analyses was conducted for each instrument used in the study. Separate reliability coefficients were calculated for each of the instruments, except the modified California High School Substance Abuse Survey (Skager, Fisher, & Maddahian, 1986), which had previously been used in a study of young adult Latinos (Cervantes, Gilbert, Salgado de Snyder, & Padilla, 1990). Alpha could not be calculated for the Traumatic Violence Severity Scale due to missing data, and certain items on the instrument that were not applicable led to the lack of sufficient data on which to conduct a reliability analysis.

The respective alpha reliability (Cronbach and Kuder Richardson) was obtained for each instrument subscale. The Gang Identification Scale (Mancillas, 1986), composed of 8 items, was found to be a reliable measure with this sample, with coefficient alpha of .74. The Social Support Index, composed of 17 items, obtained an alpha reliability coefficient of 0.52. This measure may not be a reliable indicator of social support among Latino gang members, and results have been interpreted cautiously. The Mississippi Scale for Combat Related PTSD (35 items) was found to be a reliable measure of PTSD among Latino gang members, with an alpha coefficient of .74. The Traumatic Violence Severity Scale (Gallers, 1984) was analyzed for reliability, and the 12 items were found to have an alpha of .74.

Analyses of the nine subscales of the BSI were also obtained with the following alpha levels: BSIsom (somatic), $\alpha = .78$; BSIoc (obsessive/compulsive), $\alpha = .77$; BSIint (interpersonal sensitivity), $\alpha = .71$;

BSIdep (depression), α = .71; BSIanx (anxiety), α = .69; BSIhos (hostility), α = .75; BSIphob (phobia), α = .74; BSIpar (paranoia), α = .49; BSIpsy (psychoticism), α = .48. All subscales of the BSI were found to be reliable measures of psychological symptomatology, with the exception of the BSIpar (paranoia) and the BSIpsy (psychoticism) subscales. These scales obtained low reliability coefficients, thereby suggesting they may not represent reliable subscales for this sample.

Results

Demographic Information

In order to meet the requirements of the study, only the data from the 126 subjects who stated that they were in a gang were used, resulting in a total of 81 subjects between the ages of 14 and 18 years. The remaining subjects not qualified for use in the study consisted of 5 white youths (2 reported to be non-gang identified), 1 Asian youth (non-gang identified), 5 multiracial youths (3 non-gang identified), and 29 black youths (5 non-gang identified). Of the Latino participants 94% self-reported to be gang identified, and 6% (5 youths) did not self-identify as gang members.

After being adjudicated, the subjects were serving their sentence in one of two Los Angeles Probation Camps (Camp Karl Holton or Camp Routh). Data concerning gang involvement and criminal history were obtained from the Los Angeles County Probation Camp files for 70 participants. Fifty-seven different gangs from around Los Angeles County were represented. There were a total of 88 different offenses for which gang members had been arrested, leading up to and including their current offense. The most common charge made against the subjects was Assault with a Deadly Weapon (48 offenses); Taking a Vehicle without the Owner's Consent was the second most common (44 offenses). Grand Theft Auto and Vandalism were the next most frequently cited charges, with 31 and 30 offenses, respectively. Combined alcohol and other drug violations totaled 30.

In terms of the racial/ethnic breakdown the sample consisted of 2.5% Puerto Ricans (2), 2.5% Cubans (2), 11.1% Central Americans (9), 1.2% South Americans (1), 80.2% Mexicans (65), and 2.5% missing data (2). Out of all the Latino subjects, 59.5% answered that they were born in the United States (47), 33% stated that they were born in Mexico (26), and 7.5% stated that they were born in Central America (6). Of the 78 subjects, 68% stated that their fathers were born in Mexico (53), 19% stated that their fathers were born in the United States (15), 12% stated their fathers were born in Central America (9), and 1% stated his father was born in the Philippines (1). Of the 78 subjects, 69% stated their mothers were born in Mexico (54), 18% stated their mothers were born in the United States (14), 12% stated their mothers were born in Central America (9), and 1% stated his mother was born in Argentina (1).

The mean age for the 81 subjects was 16.2 years. The youngest subject was 14 years old and the oldest was 18 years old. Of the 79 who answered the question on last school grade completed, the average was 9th grade. The lowest grade completed was 4th grade and the highest grade completed was 12th grade. The majority of the subjects (43 of the 54 who answered the question) stated their monthly household income was either less than or equal to $2,000, with 11 subjects stating their monthly household income was greater than $2,000.

Gang Involvement

Five years was the average time the subjects reported having been gang involved. The 77 subjects who responded to this question reported the minimum length of time of gang identification as 6 months, and the maximum length of time was 13 years. The percentage of immediate family members also involved in gang activity at some time was rather high. For example, 12% of the subjects reported their fathers as having been gang involved; 54% reported a brother to be gang involved; and 54% reported a cousin to be gang involved. Interestingly, 26% reported a sister to be gang involved at some time.

Substance Use

Of the 68 subjects who stated the age of first use (alcohol or other drugs), the youngest was 7 years old and the oldest was 17 years old. Average age of first use was 12 years. In terms of the effects of gang identification on alcohol and drug use, 48% of the 81 subjects (39) were found to be drinking more alcohol after they got involved in gangs; 47% (38) were drinking the same amount of alcohol as before they became involved in gangs; and 5% (4) of subjects stated they were drinking less alcohol than before they joined the gang. Of the 80 subjects who answered the questions concerning the influence of gang identification on drug use, 43% (35) used more drugs than preceding their gang identification; 52% (42) used the same quantity of drugs as preceding their gang identification;and 5% stated that they used drugs less following their gang identification.

Frequency of alcohol and drug use was based on 7 levels, ranging from 0 = Never to 6 = More than once a day. The average frequency of alcohol use was once a week, as was the average reported frequency of drug use. Polysubstance was common, with an average of four types of drugs being used in this sample.

Relationship of PTSD to Psychological Symptomatology and Exposure to Violence

A correlation matrix was created to examine any significant relationships between variables. The variable that correlated most highly with PTSD symptomatology was the obsessive/compulsive subscale of the BSI, $r = .54$, $p<.001$. In addition, all of the nine subscales of the BSI were found to have a significant relationship to PTSD symptomatology: anxiety, $r = .50$, $p<.001$; somatic, $r = .49$, $p<.001$; phobia, $r = .47$, $p<.001$; hostility, $r = .45$, $p<.001$; depression, $r = .44$, $p<.001$; interpersonal sensitivity, $r = .40$, $p<.001$; psychoticism, $r = .39$, $p<.001$; and paranoia, $r = .38$, $p<.001$.

PTSD symptomatology was also significantly correlated with frequency of exposure to traumatic violence, $r = .53$, $p<.001$. Those subjects reporting frequent exposure to gang-related violence were much more likely to also report increased PTSD symptoms.

The frequency of traumatic violence variable was also found to be significantly correlated with six of the nine subscales of the BSI: obsessive/compulsive, $r = .34$, $p<.01$; somatic, $r = .31$, $p<.01$; interpersonal sensitivity, $r = 23$, $p<05$, anxiety, $r = .22$, $p<.05$.

Relationship of Gang Identification to Alcohol and Other Drug Use

The variables that were most highly correlated with gang identification were the amount of drug use and the number of drugs used $r = .49$, $p<.001$ and $r = .49$, $p<.001$, respectively. The variable of alcohol use was also directly related to gang identification $r = .39$, $p<.001$. A significant negative relationship was found between symptoms of depression and gang identification, $r = .24$, $p<.05$. Finally, the amount of

traumatic violence gang members are exposed to significantly correlates with degree of gang identification, $r = .33$, $p<.01$.

Relationship of Drug Use to Frequency of Traumatic Violence and Psychological Symptomatology

No significant relationships were obtained between amount of drugs
used and any psychological symptomatology. However, the frequency
of exposure to traumatic violence was found to have a significant
correlation to number of drugs used, $r = .31$, $p<.01$, suggesting that, as
expected, drugs play an important role in one's willingness to engage
in gang violence. While actual amount of drug use was unrelated to
psychological symptoms, the number of drugs used (i.e., polysubstance
use) was correlated with somatic symptoms: somatic, $r = .29$, $p = .01$;
obsessive/compulsive symptoms, $r = .31$, $p<.01$; and anxiety, $r = .24$,
$p<.05$.

Multiple Regression Analyses

Multiple Regressions were conducted to assess the best predictor for
the dependent variable PTSD and the best predictor among the BSI
subscales. The first Multiple Regression included all the variables
utilized in the study. Most of the missing data was on the variables
severity of exposure to traumatic violence, income, and country of
birth. Forty-eight subjects were included in this first regression analysis. In order to assess the best predictor of PTSD symptomatology with
the largest number of subjects, a second Stepwise Multiple Regression
was conducted, excluding the variables income and country of birth.
Seventy-eight subjects were included in the second regression. Finally,
a multiple aggression was conducted to specifically assess the best
predictor for PTSD symptomatology among the nine subscales of the
Brief Symptom Inventory.
The first Stepwise Multiple Regression was conducted using the
following predictor variables: frequency of exposure to traumatic violence; severity of exposure to traumatic violence; social support; age;
alcohol use; drug use; number of drugs used; gang involvement; income; and country of birth. Frequency of exposure to traumatic violence was found to be the best predictor for PTSD among Latino gang
members, $R^2 = .30$, $\beta = .44$.

A second Stepwise Multiple Regression was conducted with the following variables: frequency of exposure to traumatic violence; social support; age; alcohol use; drug use; number of drugs used; and gang involvement. The best predictor variable of PTSD was frequency of exposure to traumatic violence, $R^2 = .29$, $\beta = .46$. The second variable to enter the equation was the number of drugs used, $R^2 = .33$, $\beta = .21$.

The third Stepwise Multiple Regression was conducted on all 81 subjects to examine the best predictor variable of PTSD among the nine subscales of the BSI. The best predictor variable for PTSD was found to be the obsessive/compulsive subscale, $R^2 = .29$, $\beta = .38$. For the anxiety subscale, $R^2 = .35$, $\beta = .29$.

Implications for Community/Clinical Interventions

It is hoped that the findings of this study will provide information to mental health professionals and others in the community for the purpose of developing effective prevention and intervention programs for gang members. It is clear that focusing all the energy on the punishment of gang members will not eradicate the problem of gang violence. The reasons for the existence of gangs are long-standing and complex and must be addressed from many different levels. It is highly unlikely that gangs will ever be extinguished, as they meet many of the needs of today's youth that have not been met either by others in the community or by society at large.

From the literature on the effects of combat on Vietnam veterans, it is clear that people who are exposed to traumatic violence, as both victims and perpetrators, can develop symptoms consistent with the diagnosis of Posttraumatic Stress Disorder. It is important to note that PTSD symptoms can manifest differently among different individuals. There are tremendous differences in values, beliefs, and convictions that people of different ethnic or racial backgrounds may hold, which may affect the expression of PTSD. Parson (1985) stated that black and Chicano soldiers from the Vietnam war suffered greater post-combat stress reactions for longer periods than did their white counterparts. This was attributed in part to the strong identification with the devalued Vietnamese people. The racism, discrimination, and "systematic exclusion" of minorities in this country added to the cumulative trauma they incurred and the identification with the Vietnamese people they experienced.

Gang violence is still predominantly directed to those similar in ethnic or racial background. On some level it is likely that a similar dynamic of identification among different gang members of similar ethnic minority status may cause an increase in the severity of stress experienced.

It appears from the literature that the experience of combat in a war situation or through violent activities may increase the violent behavior of an individual. Combat veterans have been found to be significantly more violent than either noncombat veterans or nonveterans (Boulanger & Kadushin, 1986). Horowitz and Solomon (1978) stated that it is difficult for some violent veterans to control impulses when real violence occurs; when human beings are dehumanized or devalued; and when reality and fantasy images are confused. Among gang members it is possible that the exposure to violence and the expression of PTSD symptoms through flashbacks may contribute to their further involvement in violence.

For both Vietnam veterans and gang members, it is common for life-and-death situations of war and other life-threatening situations to potentially bond people together (Wilson & Zigelbaum, 1985). Among gang members, it is clear that gang loyalty is an important element that keeps the gang together. Vietnam veterans (Wilson & Zigelbaum, 1985), and possibly gang members, as well, adhere tightly to the "warrior role," in fear that if they give up this role, they will not know how to act or respond.

Among Vietnam veterans and gang members, the ability to trust and develop close intimate relationships may be difficult. Defenses that are vital to the personality structure in combat situations can and often do lead people to distance and alienate themselves from others. In combat conditions for Vietnam veterans and gang members, survival mobilizes defenses in order to protect oneself. Bustamante and colleagues (1990) examined the psychological characteristics of gang members, all of whom disclosed that trust in others was difficult for them to establish.

From the present study, it appears that gang members, though known to victimize others, are also victims of the violence within society. The symptoms they exhibit are consistent with the diagnosis of PTSD. Hence, it is important for not only the criminal justice, probation, and mental health systems but also the community to be aware of and alert to symptomatology related to PTSD. Appropriate clinical assessments and evaluations that examine PTSD symptomatology can lead to more effective treatment for gang members suffering from PTSD, thereby reducing their potential for future mental health problems, including violent behavior.

References

Abrahamsen, D. (1960). *The psychology of crime*. New York: Columbia University Press.
Adler, P., Ovando, C., & Hocevar, D. (1984). Familiar correlates of gang membership. *Hispanic Journal of Behavioral Sciences, 6*(1), 6-76.
American Psychiatric Association (APA). (1987). *Diagnostic and statistical manual of mental disorders (DSM-III-R)* (3rd ed., rev.). Washington, DC: Author.
Andry, R. G. (1960). *Delinquency and parental pathology*. London: Methuen.
Boulanger, G., & Kadushin, C. (1986). *The Vietnam veteran redefined: Fact and fiction*. New York: Lawrence Erlbaum.
Bowker, L. H., & Klein, M. W. (1983). The etiology of female juvenile delinquency and gang membership: A test of psychological and social structural explanations. *Adolescents, 58*(72), 739-751.
Bustamante, A. L., Thomas, C. S., & James, C. B. (1990). *Psychological characteristics of gang members*. Paper presented at The National Conference on Substance Abuse and Gang Violence, November 1989.
California Council on Criminal Justice. (1986, January). *State task force on youth gang violence*. Sacramento: Author.
Cartwright, D. S., Tomson, B., & Schwartz, H. (1975). *Gang delinquency*. Monterey, CA: Brooks/Cole.
Catherall, D. R. (1986, Fall). The support system and amelioration of PTSD in Vietnam veterans. *Psychotherapy, 23*(3), 472-482.
Cervantes, R. C., Gilbert, M. J., Salgado de Snyder, V. N., & Padilla, A. M. (1990). Psychosocial and cognitive correlates of alcohol use in young adult U.S. born and immigrant Hispanics. *International Journal of the Addictions, 25*(5a/6a, 687-708).
Cervantes, R. C., Salgado de Snyder, V. N., & Padilla, A. M. (1989). Posttraumatic stress in immigrants from Central America and Mexico. *Hospital and Community Psychiatry, 40*(6), 615-619.
Collins, H. C. (1979). Street gangs. In New York City Police Department, *Profiles for Police* (pp. 14-55). New York: New York City Police Department.
Daum, J. M., & Bieliauskas, V. J. (1983). Fathers' absence and moral development of male delinquents. *Psychological Reports, 53*, 223-228.
Derogatis, L. (1975). *The brief symptom Inventory*. Maryland: Clinical Psychometric Research, Inc.
Gallers, J. (1984). *Pre- and post-combat measures of selected adjustment variables in Vietnam veterans with posttraumatic stress disorder*. Unpublished doctoral dissertation, California School of Professional Psychology, Los Angeles.
Glueck, S., & Glueck, E. T. (1968). *Delinquents and nondelinquents in perspective*. Cambridge, MA: Harvard University Press.
Hall, H. V., & Hall, F. L., III. (1987). Posttraumatic stress disorder as legal defense in criminal trials. *American Journal of Forensic Psychology, 5*(4), 45-53.

134   Psychological Effects of Violence

Helzer, J. E., Robins, L. N., & McEvoy, L. (1987). Posttraumatic stress disorder in the general population: Findings of the epidemiologic cachement area survey. *The New England Journal of Medicine*, 1630-1634.

Hoffer, T. A. (1991). *A measure of posttraumatic stress disorder among Latino gang members*. Unpublished doctoral dissertation, California School of Professional Psychology, Los Angeles.

Horowitz, M. J., & Solomon, G. (1978). Delayed stress response syndromes in Vietnam veterans. In C. R. Figley (Ed.), *Stress disorders among Vietnam veterans*. New York: Brunner/Mazel.

Keane, T. M., Caddell, J. M., & Taylor, K. L. (1988). Mississippi scale for combat-related posttraumatic stress disorder: Three studies in reliability and validity. *Journal of Consulting and Clinical Psychology, 56*(1), 85-90.

Klein, M. W. (1971). *Street gangs and street workers*. Englewood Cliffs, NJ: Prentice-Hall.

Krisberg, B. (1974, Spring). Gang youth and hustling: The psychology of survival. *Issues in Criminology, 9*, 115-131.

Lucking, R. G. (1986). Bipolar disorder in posttraumatic stress disorder—a difficult diagnosis: Care reports. *Military Medicine, 151*, 282-284.

Mancillas, P. J. (1986). *Measurement of cultural life styles, cultural transmutation, and gang identification in Mexican American adolescents*. Unpublished doctoral dissertation, California School of Professional Psychology, Los Angeles.

Martinez, M. E., Hays, J. R., & Solway, K. S. (1979). Comparative study of delinquent and non-delinquent Mexican-American youths. *Psychological Reports, 44*, 215-221.

McCubbin, H. I., Patterson, J., & Glynn, T. (1982). The social support index. In H. I. McCubbin & A. I. Thomppson (Eds.), *Family assessment inventories for research and practice*. Madison: University of Wisconsin Press.

Moore, J. W. (1990). Variations in violence among Hispanic gangs. In J. F. Kraus, S. B. Sorenson, & P. D. Juarez (Eds.), *Research conference on violence and homicide in Hispanic communities*. Los Angeles: UCLA Publication Services.

Morales, A. (1987). The Mexican-American gang member: Evaluation and treatment. In R. M. Becerra, M. Karno, & J. I. Escobar, (Eds.), *Mental health and Hispanic Americans*. New York: Grune & Stratton.

Parson, E. R. (1985). Ethnicity and traumatic stress: The intersecting point in psychotherapy. In C. R. Figley (Ed.), *Trauma and its wake: The study and treatment of posttraumatic stress disorder*. New York: Brunner/Mazel.

Rocha-Perez, D. (1989). *Hispanic gangs*. Paper presented at the conference, Troubled Youth In Troubled Times, Los Angeles.

Singer, S. I. (1981). Homogeneous victim-offender populations: A review and some research implications. *The Journal of Criminal Law and Criminology, 72*(2), 779-788.

Skager, R., Fisher, D. G., & Maddahian, E. (1986). *A statewide survey of drug and alcohol use among California students in grades 7, 9 and 11*. Sacramento: Office of the Attorney General, Crime Prevention Center.

Solkoff, N., Gray, P., & Keill, S. (1986). Which Vietnam veterans develop posttraumatic stress disorders? *The Journal of Clinical Psychology, 42*(5), 687-698.

Stonequist, E. B. (1937). *The marginal man*. New York: Scribner.

U.S. Department of Justice, Bureau of Justice Statistics. (1988). *Drug use and crime*. Washington, DC: Author.

Vigil, J. D. (1990). *Street socialization, locura behavior, and violence among Chicano gang members*. In J. F. Kraus, S. B. Sorenson, & P. D. Juarez (Eds.), Research conference on violence and homicide in Hispanic communities. Los Angeles: UCLA Publication Services.

Wilson, J. P. (1988). Understanding the Vietnam veteran. In F. M. Ochberg, *Post-traumatic therapy and victims of violence*. New York: Brunner/Mazel.

Wilson, J. P., & Zigelbaum, S. D. (1985). Posttraumatic stress disorder and the disposition to criminal behavior. In C. R. Figley (Ed.), Trauma and its wake: Traumatic stress theory, research and intervention. Vol. II. New York: Brunner/Mazel.

Yablonsky, L. (1962.) *The violent gang*. New York: Macmillan.

9

Survivors' Response to Gang Violence

NORMA C. JOHNSON
SAUNDREA D. YOUNG

Introduction

During the month of September 1989 there were 48 murders in 28 days. This did not happen in El Salvador, Lebanon, or Belfast; this happened in an area known as South Central Los Angeles. By the end of that year there had been more than 300 murders committed in South Central Los Angeles. This represents more deaths per year than many major cities have in 5 years. By mid-December 1991 there had been 354 lives lost to homicide. Of this number 123 were classified by the Los Angeles Police Department gang unit as "gang-related homicides." The term *gang-related* is defined by the *Los Angeles Police Office of Operations Manual* (Los Angeles Police Department, 1990) in the following manner:

> *Gang Related Crime:* Any of the below listed crimes where the suspect is identified in the department files as a gang member.
> *Gang Motivated Crime:* Any of the below listed crimes where the victim or suspect is an active gang member and the crime occurs due to that membership (e.g., a suspect shouts a gang affiliation)
> Homicide, robbery, kidnapping, arson, weapons law violations, rape/attempted rape, shooting into an inhabited dwelling, intimidation of a witness, extortion, felonious assault, assault/battery on a police officer, sale, distribution, possession of controlled substance.

Given the broad definition of gang-related/gang-motivated crime, it is not always possible to confine a homicide to the preceding definition. In some cases the suspect or victim may be a gang member, but the homicide may have nothing to do with either the membership or the affiliation. For example Ms. Smith was killed by her boyfriend, the father of her child, who was a member of the Crips gang. The murder could be classified as the result of a domestic dispute. Ms. Smith was attempting to end the relationship with this man and was seeing someone else, yet her boyfriend was not going to let her go. He burst into the house where she lived with her family and began shooting everyone in sight, killing her immediately. It was classified as a domestic dispute *and* gang-related because of the suspect's gang membership. Homicides will frequently be classified under more than one motive, based on the circumstances.

What happens to the families? What happens to their lives? What happens to the children who are affected by these losses? How do they pick up their lives and go on? One answer has been early intervention with counseling and with strong community support. Another answer has been the education of the public about the impact of this type of crime and the effects it has on the community. This effort has been effectively carried out by volunteers, concerned citizens, and the survivors themselves.

This chapter will discuss the strategy that was utilized to develop a full service program for the families and loved ones of homicide victims. The need for intervention with counseling and supportive services is not only necessary for the recovery of the individual who has been the victim of this violent loss, but is also therapeutic for the community. Homicide and its impact are unlike any other sudden loss. The grief from this particular loss has far-reaching consequences for everyone involved with the identified client. Appropriate treatment should include thorough assessment of the circumstances surrounding the homicide and the client's exposure to the actual events .

Grief Theory

The application of grief theory as it relates to the loss of loved ones from violence is a relatively new field of exploration. Much of the written material about grief is based on the work by Dr. Elizabeth Kübler-Ross. Her work with terminally ill patients resulted in the well-noted identification and description of the various stages of grief and is referred to as "grief work." This grief work is similarly replicated when the loss is traumatic, however the differences are significant and require discussion.

1. Shock and Denial

The first reaction to any tragedy is usually met with a numbing shock and denial. According to Kübler-Ross these reactions function as a buffer after unexpected ego-dystonic news, and allow the survivor to draw on the emotional resources needed to move through the grieving process. In time, other less radical defenses are utilized. This stage of grief, as described by Kübler-Ross (1969), usually employs temporary defenses. However, within the context of homicide, it has been noted that both the nature of the death and the circumstances surrounding it significantly impact the survivors' ability to move through the temporary phase.

Example 1. Ms. Jones's 13-year-old daughter, Lisa, left the house with an older friend, Jean, to get a hamburger from a nearby stand. Ms. Jones was fairly new to the neighborhood, but had talked with Jean on several occasions and judged her to be of good character. Ms. Jones had no misgivings about granting Lisa permission to go with her friend. Fifteen minutes later Ms. Jones heard several shots, but because of the frequency of gunplay in the area, thought no more about it. Shortly thereafter, a neighbor appeared at her door to inform her that both Lisa and Jean had been shot. Ms. Jones arrived at the crime scene and witnessed her daughter dying from multiple gunshot wounds. When Lisa was pronounced dead at the scene, Ms. Jones recounts that "all went black." She describes that period as feeling "on automatic." She was able to participate in the funeral arrangements, but felt "unattached," as if she were "watching a scene from a movie." For Ms. Jones, both the shock of witnessing her child die and the denial of the loss increased the time spent in this phase of the grief process.

Example 2. Ms. Williams's son, Jerry, was killed in a drive-by shooting incident while visiting a friend. Immediately after she was notified of his death, Ms. Williams collapsed and was hospitalized in the Intensive Care Unit for several weeks with acute diabetic and cardiac symptoms. During this period Ms. Williams could not tolerate any mention of Jerry's name or participate in final arrangements. When the funeral took place, Ms. Williams' condition was too critically emotional for her to leave the hospital.

2. Anger

The next response to the loss is expressed with anger, which is vented in a variety of ways. Many survivors are angry at God, at hospital personnel, at law enforcement, at the perpetrator, and, most important, at themselves (guilt reaction). In addition their anger is often displaced onto persons who are in proximity, but cannot understand what they are experiencing—for example, employers, best friends, other family members, and so on. Anger is vented at persons who still have their loved ones and are insensitive to the survivors' preoccupation with their loss.

Example 3. After the death of her son, Alex, Ms. Black was so outraged that the man who killed him was given a light sentence that she often had fantasies about how she would kill him when he was released. Even though she was at no risk for acting upon her impulse, she stated she had to do something with all her anger.

3. Isolation

Survivors frequently experience themselves as being isolated from all of their support systems. Their perception that friends and acquaintances are uncomfortable or unable to discuss the loss often is grounded in reality. Friends *are* often afraid of the violence, unpredictability, and closeness of the act. Knowing that it happened to someone they love often makes them fearful of contamination. In addition, friends may not be sensitive enough or skilled enough to penetrate the survivors' sense of aloneness.

Example 4. Mrs. Stevens is the 79-year-old matriarch of a large extended family. Her daughter, Annette, was found murdered in a friend's car. Mrs. Stevens complained bitterly that not one family member, co-worker, or church member would let her discuss her feelings about Annette. She was always stopped by what she described as meaningless platitudes. "No one understands, no one wants to understand. I am all alone."

4. Acceptance/Recovery

The acceptance phase of the grief process is inextricably linked to the survivors' recovery. It is at this point that an ego-syntonic meaning has been ascribed to the homicide and the survivors are able to reinvest in the activities of daily living. The death and the grieving process have been satisfactorily incorporated by the survivors and they are free to productively move on.

Example 5. Ms. Thomas's 17-year-old college-bound son was killed in a drive-by shooting while he stood on his front lawn. Ms. Thomas's abiding faith in God enabled her to affix meaning to her son's death. She was, she felt, to use this experience to help other youths confront the issues of black-on-black crime. She began by giving a presentation to various youth groups about the death of her son. Later she became involved in an impact program that allowed her to go directly into the penal system and address young men who were incarcerated for gang activity. She stated that her "therapy" was watching the shift in expression on the faces of the young men as she told them her story. Through this effort she was able to actively participate in her recovery by making possible a change in the attitudes of some young gang members.

Community Level Response

South Central Los Angeles is a community with major economic and social problems. A primary concern within this community has always been in developing skills that allow for surviving the external threats that pose immediate harm to a person's existence. However, in the early 1980s a major increase in violence took place in the city, and South Central Los Angeles was hit extremely hard. This increase in crime brought a record number of homicides. The residents began to view this crisis as an *internal* threat that must be dealt with from within the community. The initial response from the community to this constant loss of life was shock, followed by a realization that something had to be done for the families who were facing these losses. The residents of South Central Los Angeles were aware that survivors in other communities had become involved in efforts to support one another through the crisis of homicide. However this effort had not been duplicated in South Central Los Angeles and it posed a major challenge to the community. The first author, serving as a Victims' Advocate for the City Attorney's Victims Assistance Program, was eager to formulate a vehicle to allow the pain and anguish witnessed on a daily basis to be resolved.

Thus, in April 1985 the Loved Ones of Homicide Victims support group was founded by this author and many of the survivors and concerned residents of South Central Los Angeles. They, having been affected by the loss of a relative or friend from a homicide, understood that others were suffering as much as they were. They recognized that there could be comfort in the togetherness and sharing of pain. The support group, publicized by word of mouth, met once a month on Saturdays in an office of the Southern Christian Leadership Conference. The tears were many and the pain was riveting. Many of the survivors shared similar experiences of the anxiety and frustration they felt with the system. Others discussed the insensitivity they experienced from people who did not understand their agony. During this first year the survivors began speaking out against the tragedy of homicide and the effect it was having on the community.

On March 17, 1986, an article in the *Los Angeles Times* described the efforts of the group's members to support one another through the tragedy of homicide. The article caught the attention of the social work staff of the Martin Luther King, Jr., County Hospital, since many of the victims were taken to county facilities in critical condition and later succumbed to their injuries. The staff, after breaking the news of the patients' death to the families would have nowhere to refer the families for continued support. The second author was Assistant Director of Hospital Social Service at Martin Luther King, Jr., Hospital. She contacted concerned personnel at the hospital and the organizers of the support group, in a effort to develop a full-service therapeutic program for survivors.

The support group incorporated, and the nonprofit Loved Ones of Homicide Victims (LOHV) Service Center was created. Several licensed therapists made a commitment to provide counseling services on a volunteer basis. The support group relocated to the Sunnyside Baptist Church, as this site was offered free of charge by Reverend F. D. Bullock and his congregation. Locating the Service Center within a church permitted the successful integration of a culturally relative treatment model for psychological counseling and also allowed the clients to see that their religious beliefs need not be compromised by their seeking professional help.

Treatment and Services

The Service Center currently provides individual, family, and group therapy for a range of psychological problems ranging from depression to post-traumatic stress disorder. The method of treatment is determined by the needs as they are assessed by the clinical staff. Clients who cope by sharing with and supporting others may choose group treatment. These clients need only to know that they are not alone in the feelings they are experiencing.

Individual therapy is the choice of those clients who have a more intense and personal need to incorporate the homicide into an acceptable event in their lives. Family sessions enable each member to address and adjust to the loss while strengthening and supporting their relationships. The support group is open-ended and client-centered. The sessions convene twice a month and are facilitated by licensed therapists serving as facilitators.

The discussions range from the shock and senselessness of the murder to the insensitivity of the police and criminal justice system. Many of the "senior" survivors will in very short order find themselves supporting "new" survivors and helping them understand the depth of the pain and loss through sharing their own experience. The survivors form a bond with each other immediately. The support from this bond helps them cope with key periods, such as holidays, anniversaries, and birthdays.

Supportive Services

The Center also provides the survivors with a range of supportive social services that assist them, both financially and emotionally, through the adjustment period. These services are funded by the California State Office of Criminal Justice Planning and by a Los Angeles City Community Development grant along with private donations.

Emergency Assistance: This component provides emergency food, shelter, and cash advances to assist with the burial of the victim.

Court Support: This component connects the client with resources available within the Victims Assistance Program. Many clients want to be involved in the criminal court proceedings after the perpetrators are apprehended, but often are not aware of the process. This component works with the family and the Victims' Advocate to ensure that the survivors are informed and supported throughout the criminal proceedings.

Family Case Management: This component identifies the services that clients may need as they continue their treatment at the Center. These services include response to referrals from schools regarding children who demonstrate behavior or academic problems, counseling regarding disruptive family issues, and planning and coordination of therapeutically designed activities.

Latino Victim Services: The Center provides bilingual, bicultural services to the Latino population in the South Central Los Angeles area. Previously the Latino victims in this area were underserved because of language and cultural barriers. This component was funded in 1990 and, without a doubt, has filled a gap in an area once overlooked. To date, the center has served the needs of 75 Latino survivors' families.

Center Volunteers

The Center has developed and employed both traditional and nontraditional methods of treatment. Again the emphasis has been to apply therapeutic principles within a cultural context. Therefore, recovery for many of the clients includes involvement at the Center in a range of activities from peer counseling to manning the Warm Line, to maintenance of the "Memory Wall." Client volunteers feel they are part of the process that is vital both to stopping the violence and to helping others who have been touched by violence in the same way.

Example 6. Ms. Brown lost her daughter in 1986. The perpetrators were never caught. Ms. Brown was seen at the Center for group treatment only and shared her painful experience with others like herself. It became very important to her that the life of her daughter and other victims not be forgotten. Ms. Brown, along with other survivors, developed the "Memory Wall" and began the tradition of placing pictures of the victims on the Center bulletin board. For Ms. Brown this was a way of not ever forgetting the ones who were gone, but also served as a way for her to face the reality of her loss. The "Memory Wall" was her therapeutic project. Although the "Memory Wall" is a permanent part of the Center, Ms. Brown is no longer actively involved with it. On occasion she will visit the Center, however she has moved through the grieving process and has gone on with her life.

Client volunteers are involved in various Center projects. Important events are the Thanksgiving and Christmas food baskets, which are made up from food and financial donations solicited by the volunteers, and the annual Christmas party, which has grown each year. Many of the clients participate in the development of the Christmas program and the solicitation of the donations for toys. The work of the client volunteers, in collaboration with the board of directors and the staff, has turned the Christmas party into a major community event.

LOHV Service Center has been successful in recruiting volunteers. Since its inception, the nature of the work has interested various groups in the community. Prominent African-American women, many of them judges and lawyers, have hosted fund-raisers for the Center, with proceeds going to a special program at the Center. These groups have also become the primary source for our food baskets during the Thanksgiving and Christmas seasons.

The most innovative volunteer project to date has been the Victims Impact Program. Two client volunteers participate with the California Youth Authority at Fred C. Nellis School by sharing their experience with the wards and inmates in the facility. The women involved in this program have both lost a child to homicide. For them therapy included reaching out to those responsible for their pain and anguish. Because of their commitment to share with these young men the impact of violence on them, both women have made extraordinary sacrifices, including taking time off from work without pay to appear in these classes. Their presentations frequently utilize pictures of their own children in life and death. For many of the wards this is their first encounter with a victim or family member. Both the client volunteers and the inmates involved this program seem to be benefiting from this form of treatment, which in the future will be developed as a model for prevention.

Children as Survivors

Children and teenagers who have experienced the loss of a relative or friend to homicide are particularly vulnerable developmentally. Children require safety, security, and constancy. Homicide disrupts all of these needs. Teenagers also require safety and security as they begin to explore and master their environment and their identity. Homicide again negatively impacts this process.

Because of their environment, circumstances, and coping capacity, many of the children and teenagers are at high risk for responding violently to their loss. Others may respond with academic and/or behavioral problems, depression, and symptoms of post-traumatic stress disorder.

Example 7. Casey is a 5-year-old male child who, one year earlier, was a percipient witness to the murder of his 10-year-old sister. Several days prior to being treated at the Center, Casey had experienced frequent unprovoked crying spells in school. The teacher also reported that he engaged in a conversation with his classmates about how he needed their help to get to heaven so he could see his sister.

Casey's mother was already receiving counseling at the Center and recognized Casey's behavior and conversation as symptoms of unresolved grief. Casey was involved in play group treatment with other children and was allowed to share his feeling about the loss of his sister. The current increase in the rate of homicides has resulted in an increase in the number of referrals from school mental health personnel, who have been made aware of the Center's program for children through presentations by the staff, the therapists, and the family case manager. Early intervention and specifically designed programs for these children are pivotal to the Center's operation.

Summary

The survivors of a homicide victim are often the only ones who can speak on behalf of the actual victim. In most cases the survivors are having their first experience with a system that is insensitive to their plight. The survivors have very limited knowledge of the criminal justice system, and much of the process of the court system has not been explained to them. Many survivors at this point simply walk away from the system; a smaller number will fight for the right to understand the process that now controls so much of their lives.

In California and in most other states, there are now programs for victims' compensation. These programs are funded by restitution funds that are generated from fines and penalties assessed against defendants. In California a victim or his or her family may be entitled to up to $46,000 in compensation for such expenses as medical costs and lost wages. If the deceased victim was the head of the household and the family was financially and legally dependent, there is compensation for funeral and burial expenses, loss of support, and reimbursement of incurred expenses related to mental health counseling.

Such groups as Parents of Murdered Children, Justice for Homicide Victims, Loved Ones of Homicide Victims came into existence because of the system's lack of response to the needs of the survivors. These groups provide a vehicle for survivors to be involved, however remotely, in the process of justice. In recent years they have impacted on legislation that reflects the needs and concerns of victims and survivors. In addition all of these groups help the survivors overcome the hopelessness and helplessness that they feel as a result of the violent act itself.

In our opinion the most important development in the area of victims' rights has been the education and empowerment of the victims themselves. We are beginning to see changes in the current laws, which automatically give the defendant advantages, because victims are making demands and are voting for the political leaders who support their cause.

The necessity for survivors to organize and participate in their own recovery from the tragedy of homicide is an area that must be explored by all of us who work and provide service to them. The experience of working with survivors and the LOHV Service Center has provided new insight into the possibilities of reducing the effects of homicide. It has also provided an opportunity to develop a culturally sensitive model for intervention and prevention.

The most rewarding aspect of our effort has been to experience the amazing recovery of some of the survivors. The model for treatment at the Center is working, a model that is based upon the commitment of the community, professionals in the field, and the survivors themselves. The proof is in the smiles and laughter that once again fill their days.

References

Kübler-Ross, E. (1969). *On death and dying*. New York: Macmillan.
Los Angeles Police Department Office of Operations. (1990). *Definition of gang-related crimes*.

10

A Working Typology of Grief Among Homicide Survivors

L. JOHN KEY

Introduction

According to Martinez, Schnell, and Waxweiler (1989), from 1968 to 1985, the rate of homicide in the United States increased 44%. More specifically, Margaret Heckler, Secretary of the Department of Health and Human Services, in a report from her task force on Black and Minority Health (1985) found approximately 59,000 excess deaths among America's blacks between 1979 and 1981.

Homicide, inflicted by another person with the intent to injure or kill, is the third leading cause of premature mortality from injury, after motor vehicle collisions and suicides (Centers for Disease Control, 1987). However, as Bard, Arnone, and Nemroff (1986) point out, most attention to this form of violence usually focuses on the loss of life and not on the consequences for the surviving relatives, even though Holmes and Masuda (1978); Danto, Brahns, and Kutscler (1982); and others have suggested that across all cultures the loss of a close family member by sudden violent means is a traumatic and stressful event in and of itself. Furthermore, Bard and colleagues and Danto and colleagues have pointed out that the ignoring of homicide survivors should be a matter of social concern, a matter of public policy in the field of mental health—especially psychiatry. Until the 1960s, psychiatrists received almost no clinical training regarding homicide or treatment of the surviving family members (Danto et al., 1982).

147

There has been very little empirical research on the grief reactions of suicidal survivors (MacIntosh & Wrobleski, 1988), and there has been even less research with homicide survivors. One of the few books on grief reaction, is that of Worden (1982), *Grief Counseling and Grief Therapy.* He devotes a full chapter to this topic, which he calls "Grieving Special Types of Losses." In addition to citing suicide, Sudden Infant Death Syndrome (SIDS), miscarriages and stillbirth, abortion, and anticipatory grief, he discusses sudden death from the perspective of homicide survivors. He also delineates some special features that should be considered when working with the survivors of a sudden death, which include such issues as guilt, blame, unreality, helplessness, and the increased need to understand why the death occurred.

Review of the Literature

The concept of the "victim" is not well defined. This concept was present even in ancient times, because it is connected closely with the idea and the practice of sacrifice. Mythological sources provide sufficient evidence to the existence of the different types of sacrifice and victims, and the symbolic elements connected to those ritual practices. The *Oxford English Dictionary* (1961) defines victim as:

a. a living creature killed and offered as a sacrifice to some deity or supernatural power;

b. a person who is put to death or subjected to torture by another; one who suffers severely in body or property through cruel or oppressive treatment; one who is reduced or destined to suffer under some oppressive or destructive agency; one who perishes or suffers in health, etc. from some enterprise or pursuit voluntarily undertaken. In weaker sense, one who suffers some injury, hardship, or loss is badly treated or taken advantage of.

In addition, there is a well-developed vocabulary in English connected with the notion of victims:

1. Victimhood: The state of being a victim.
2. Victimizable: Capable of being victimized.
3. Victimization: The action of victimizing or fact of being victimized in various senses.

4. Victimize: To make a victim, to cause to suffer inconvenience, discomfort, annoyance, etc.
5. Victimizer: One who victimizes another or others.
6. Victimless: The absence of a clearly identifiable victim other than doers. For example, a criminal solution.

It was not until the 1940s that the founders of criminology showed an interest in the victim, even though they were aware of the crucial importance of the criminal/victim relationship. For example, several researchers who studied the psychological relationship between the criminal and his victim speak to the importance of studying the criminal/victim relationship as a vehicle to understand crime and its origins and implications (Mendelsohn, 1956; Von Hentig, 1947).

However, the proponents of *victimology* have mostly focused on the primary victim and not the survivors. For example, Mendelsohn (1956a) in looking at how a subject became a victim, developed a classification system based on the degree of culpability in becoming a victim. Wolfgang (1970a) reported that 25% of murder victims precipitate their attack. He called these behaviors victim precipitated homicides. Herjonic and Meyer (1976) discovered that 15% (32 of 214) of the homicide victims studied had a psychiatric history, which was true for only 4% of the general population, suggesting some mental impairment.

Kutash (1978) developed a classification system and treatment protocol for victims. Kutash's basic aggression victimology vocabulary and classification system is as follows:

Victim (n.): someone killed, injured, or otherwise harmed by, or suffering from, some act or acts of aggression.
1. Primary victim: the person killed, injured, or otherwise harmed by an act or acts of aggression.
2. Secondary victim: the person suffering due to an act of aggression against a significant person other than themselves.

Victimage (n.): that which belongs to the state or condition of being a victim; for example, experiencing victimage.

victimal (adj.): pertaining to or concerned with victimizing.

victiming (v.): making oneself a victim; promoting victimage.

victimization (n.): the state of being victimized.

victimized (v.t.): to be made a victim of.

He went even farther and divided the victims of aggression into two distinct categories: (a) those who are victimized (play no role in becoming a victim), and (b) those who are victiming (promoting the victimization). However, he did not go into detail in discussing secondary victimage or what the treatment implications are for secondary victimage.

A Working Typology of Grief

The need to conduct additional research on the subject of homicide survivors is evident from the paucity of prior research in this area. Also, my clinical experience in grief counseling reveals the need for more published information from other clinicians on grief counseling of homicide survivors. Additional knowledge in this area will serve as a guide for the small number of clinicians who are counseling and tracking homicide survivors who are still grieving.

The investigators in homicide survivors' grief counseling noted the emergence of a recognizable conciliation of attitudes, beliefs, and emotional patterns in the survivors, which are influenced by their culture as well as the circumstances leading up to and surrounding the murder.

I have categorized these attitudes, beliefs, and emotional patterns as follows:

1. Isolated sudden murder survivor pattern
2. Drug/alcohol-related murder survivor pattern
3. Domestic violence homicide survivor pattern
4. Serial murder survivor pattern
5. Gang-related survivor pattern

All of the survivor patterns are related to secondary victimage in that each type of survivor is suffering due to an act or acts of aggression against a significant person other than themselves. However, this is the point in which the similarity seems to end.

Isolated Sudden Murder Survivor Pattern

The isolated sudden murder survivor pattern is exemplified by the survivors' feelings of unreality, exacerbation of guilt feelings, the need to blame someone for what happened, sense of helplessness, and regrets for things they did not say and/or never got around to doing with the deceased.

Drug/Alcohol-Related Murder Survivor Pattern

In the drug/alcohol-related survival pattern, the survivors usually knew that the primary victim was involved in either trafficking or using illicit drugs, but the survivors were unwilling or fearful of confronting him or her. The survivors usually had some forewarning and during this period of anticipation had actually begun the task of mourning and the various responses of grief so that when death did come, the survivors seemed almost relieved because of the inevitability of the death of the primary victim due to his or her life-style.

Domestic Violence Homicide Survivor Pattern

In the domestic violence homicide survivor pattern, there was a history of physical conflict on many occasions prior to the homicide. In fact, a survey conducted by the U.S. National Commission on the Causes and Prevention of Violence found one in four men and one in six women approving of a husband hitting his wife under certain conditions. Stark and McEvoy (1970) and Gelles (1974) found that out of 80 married individuals interviewed, 54% mentioned at least one incident of husband/wife violence in their marriage.

Therefore, the surviving family members knew of the violence and abuse, but because of the view that the family is sacred, chose not to get involved. However, the survivors might well have been able to do some anticipatory work, not unlike the drug/alcohol survivors, and may also feel some guilt for not doing enough. These survivors might have some homicidal thoughts themselves.

Serial Murder Survivor Pattern

In the serial murder survivor pattern the survivors appear to respond to the death of the loved one much like the isolated sudden murder survivors do. There is the feeling of unreality, exacerbation of guilt feelings, sense of helplessness, and regrets, but especially a need to blame themselves for not doing more to protect the victim. It should be noted that until very recently, serial murders had not been part of the Afro-American community's experience.

Gang-Related Survivor Pattern

The usual survivors are single mothers with a teenage son or sons also involved in gang activities. The primary victims were usually physically larger and stronger than the mothers and had been exhibiting conduct problems at home and school. The survivors didn't respond with a sense of unreality, usually having an expectation of "when will it happen," or "what will he get into next?" In other words, the survivors believed they had no control and, in reality, usually did not. In addition, some survivors are concerned that their sons or daughters might have been homicide perpetrators themselves.

In summary, what seems to emerge from our clinical experience is that the culture and circumstances surrounding and leading up to the murders greatly affected how survivors coped with the traumatic events.

Case Histories

The case histories described in the following pages are those with whom I worked when I had a caseload at Loved Ones of Homicide, Inc. There are, of course, other ways that such cases could be categorized and other types of homicide survivors that are not discussed. But the purpose of presenting the case histories is to sensitize the reader to the homicide victim trajectory. The names have been changed, but the circumstances surrounding the homicides are true.

Case 1: Robert P. (Isolated Sudden Murder Survivor)

Mr. Robert P. was a 55-year-old minority male who worked for a large governmental agency in the city of Los Angeles. He was reported to be a devoted husband and father. His wife, the primary victim, worked for the Postal Service. They had two children, a boy and a girl, ages 17 and 19. She was killed while delivering mail at the perpetrator's home. He watched her from a peephole in his front door as she delivered his mail. He shot her with a 12-gauge shotgun. He claimed that he had mistaken the victim for a man who had shot him in the leg 2 years earlier, even though the victim was in her postal uniform and didn't resemble the alleged assailant.

The primary victim and the survivor (Robert P.) were to have met for their regular lunch but she was killed before the lunch.

For a year and a half, Robert P. experienced feelings of unreality; for example, he left their bedroom exactly as it had been when she left that morning for work.

For a number of months, he could only cry and express guilt that he shouldn't have allowed her to go to work that particular day. At night he constantly thought of the moment when he had learned of his wife's death. In addition, he couldn't drive near the street where she was murdered for months.

Discussion: This case was classified as an isolated sudden murder because there was seemingly no reason for the murder. The primary victim just happened to be there.

Case 2: Jimmy D. (Drug/Alcohol-Related Murder Survivor)

Mr. and Mrs. D. had been married for 35 years and had three grown sons. The two older sons are very successful. The oldest son is a lawyer and the middle son is completing a degree in accounting.

Three days after Christmas the victim, the youngest son, was found dead in his apartment directly across the street from the family home. The parents and his brothers had been aware of some unusual activities at the victim's home, but had never confronted him about their concerns.

The primary victim had been somewhat of a loner all of his life. He showed the appropriate love for his family, but adamantly refused to allow them to get involved with his "business."

Discussion: The family had known for many months that this victim was possibly involved in illicit drug activity, but for various reasons, including his defensiveness, fear of his customers, and the feeling that it was inevitable that something would happen to him, they chose not to act.

Case 3: Mr. and Mrs. Kevin J. (Domestic Violence Survivor)

Annabelle was a victim of spousal abuse, and her parents had been encouraging her to leave her husband Bob for the past 5 years. He had inflicted serious injuries on her at various times, including breaking her nose and stabbing her in the arm with an ice pick. On the day of her murder, she had called her parents and asked her father to pick her up in front of the house because she was planning to leave. But this time when her husband saw her standing outside the house with her packed bags, he stabbed her in the back. She died at the scene.

Discussion: This woman had been in an abusive relationship for at least 5 years. However, for various reasons including economic, social, and psychological, she was unable to leave. The family knew of the abuse. Prior to the murder, they concluded that it was the victim's problem and if she wanted to, she could stay. In fact, her mother had commented: "She made her bed, now let her sleep in it."

Case 4: Jenny W. (Serial Murder Survivor)

Mrs. W. knew her daughter was running the streets a lot and could possibly be using drugs. Mary W., age 21, had left home 3 days before her death to go to a local club. She was found dead in a vacant house. Her body was riddled with bullets. Three other girls of approximately the same age had been murdered in the same general area.

Discussion: The mother was aware of the serial murders in the area, but didn't think that her daughter was a possible target. When the daughter's body was found, the mother had to be hospitalized, as a result of the intense guilt she suffered as well as the actual loss.

Case 5: Helen C. (Gang-Related Survivor)

On the evening of his murder, Anthony was standing under a street light talking with some other boys. A car circled the block, and before the boys could run, Anthony was shot in the head. He died at the scene, killed by a drive-by assailant.

Discussion: Mrs. C. was aware that her son, Anthony, was hanging out with the wrong crowd. The mother had sought help from a school counselor and a local social agency, to no avail. She felt totally helpless, yet anticipated the eventual outcome.

Summary on Case Histories

These topologies were not based on empirical research, but were based on clinical experiences of one investigator at a nonprofit grief counseling program in South Central Los Angeles. However, they point to the need for treatment and supportive services for survivors of homicide, treatment that should be formulated in keeping with the beliefs, values, and circumstances involved in such murders.

Treatment Issues

Parker (1972) claims that first of all, there are three basic approaches to bereavement counseling:

1. Bereavement counseling is offered to all individuals, particularly to families in which death has taken a parent or child;
2. People will recognize their need for help and reach out for assistance; and
3. If one can predict in advance who is likely to have difficulty a year or two following the loss, then one can do something, by way of early intervention, to preclude an unresolved grief reaction.

However, with any approach, the overall goal of grief therapy is to resolve the conflict of separation from the deceased to facilitate the completion of the grief. That is, the counselor wants to help the survivor complete any unfinished business with the deceased and to be able to say a final good-bye.

The influential paper on grief and bereavement, "The Symptomatology and Management of Acute Grief" was written by Lidemann (1944), following the Coconut Grove nightclub fire in which 500 people lost their lives. Afterward, Lidemann and his colleagues found from their observations of 101 bereaved patients that most of them had similar patterns, which he described as the pathologic characteristics and manifestations of normal or acute grief. He listed these as:

1. Somatic or bodily distress of some type;
2. Preoccupation with the image of the deceased;
3. Guilt relating to the deceased or circumstances of the death;
4. Hostile reactions; and
5. The inability to function as one did before the loss.

However, Parker (1972) raised some questions regarding the limitation of the study. For example, Lidemann did not present figures to show the relative frequency of the syndrome described. Also, Lidemann did not mention how many interviews he had with the patients and how much time had passed between the date of the loss and the interviews.

Before one can fully comprehend the impact of a loss and the human behavior associated with loss, Bowlby (1980) argues that one must have some understanding of the meaning of attachment. Bowlby contends that human beings tend to make strong affectionate bonds with others, and strong emotional reactions occur when those bonds are threatened or broken.

Furthermore, Bowlby argues that these attachments occur in both animals and humans. He relates the work of Lorenz with animals and Harlow's work with young monkeys. Bowlby's thesis is that these attachments come from a need for security and safety; they develop early in life, are usually directed toward a few specific individuals, and tend to endure throughout much of the life cycle. Therefore, forming attachment with significant others is considered normal behavior not only for the child but also for the adult.

In addition, Engel (1961) argues that the loss of a loved one is psychologically traumatic to the same extent as being severely wounded or burned. Furthermore, he contends that grief represents a departure from the normal state of health and well-being, and just as healing is necessary in the physical realm in order to bring the body back into homeostatic balance, a period of time is likewise needed to return the mourner to a similar state of equilibrium.

Following Engel's approach, after one sustains a loss, there are certain tasks of mourning that must be accomplished for equilibrium to be reestablished and for the process of mourning to be completed.

Worden (1982) identified the four major tasks of mourning. They are as follows:

1. To accept the reality of the loss;
2. To experience the pain of grief;
3. To adjust to an environment in which the deceased is missing; and
4. To withdraw emotional energy and reinvest in another relationship.

However, Worden points out that one has to make the distinction between the terms *mourning*, to indicate the process that occurs after a loss, and *grief*, which refers to the personal experience of the loss. In addition, since mourning is seen as a process, it is appropriate to view it in terms of stages. Many people writing on the subject of grief have listed up to 9 stages of grief and at least one lists 12. However, the problem is that people do not necessarily pass through stages in the order they are given.

In his work, Parker (1970) defines four phases of mourning. They are as follows:

1. The period of numbness, which occurs close to the time of the loss;
2. The period of yearning for the deceased;
3. The period of disorganization and despair; and
4. The period of reorganized behavior.

Therefore, it appears that for both practitioners and paraprofessionals, the primary goal of grief therapy is to resolve the conflicts of separation from the deceased and to complete the grief task. However, given the fact that the circumstances leading up to and surrounding the act of homicide specifically influence the presentation of subsequent bereavement, it is important to not only make a sound assessment of the circumstances prior to beginning therapy, but also have some sensitivity to the culture. For example, we have found in certain cases, such as with drug-related survivors and domestic violence cases, that survivors may have already begun the anticipatory work of letting go once they realized the victims were on a possible homicidal trajectory. On the other hand, the isolated sudden murder survivors or the serial murder survivors may be in total shock concerning the murder.

Conclusions

The idea of a possible working typology of homicide survivors came from the work of MacIntosh and Wrobleski (1988). As with grief reactions among suicide survivors, there has been little research focused upon those who survive the homicidal death of a family member.

The purpose of these case studies and possible theoretical formulation is to investigate how circumstances leading up to and surrounding the murder do affect the grief work of the survivor.

This is especially true in the Afro-American community, where the attitude and behavior of Afro-Americans in regard to death cannot be adequately understood without reference to the accompanying persistent historical presence of violent death (Kalish & Reynolds, 1976).

In fact, one student's account of the grim reality of sudden death in the Afro-American community follows:

Death in my own home ghetto is all too sudden and very seldom peaceful. A teenager was once walking through a housing project on his way home. Suddenly, without warning, a bullet shattered his skull. A man has crawled down a street and died as his fellow citizens stumbled over his body. Children playing in vacant lots and fields have found the bodies of dead men and women, mutilated and left to rot. Death is common and violent in a class of people held prisoner by the invisible chains of racism. (Carter, 1971)

Therefore, to be Afro-American in America is to be a part of a history told in terms of contact with death and coping with death. The theme of death permeates early spirituals, novels, music and song, and the encounter with death is personal.

Kalish and colleagues, (1976) found that the Afro-Americans they interviewed for their study revealed they had more contact with those who had died during the 2 years than respondents in other cultural groups. This chapter contends that because of the permeation of the death theme in the Afro-American community, this has to affect the grief work. Therefore, the clinician working with an Afro-American client or, for that matter, a Hispanic-American, an Asian/Pacific Islander, or a member of any other cultural group, would be well advised to investigate the circumstances leading up to the murder of a family member. If the family members have already begun anticipatory work prior to the death, the treating clinicians need to take that into consideration when they are interviewing the clients and not expect the clients to be experiencing intense feelings of numbness and unreality as they would with an isolated sudden murder.

It is important to meet the clients where they are in the grief process— a process that may in fact be dictated by the circumstances leading up to and surrounding the murder. This is in contrast to assuming that every client has to passively go through the various stages. In addition, the clinician has to be very careful in forming a therapeutic rapport with clients from some minority communities where there may not be a great deal of motivation for treatment beyond the initial crisis phase due to some suspiciousness toward psychology, psychiatry, and counseling in general.

References

Bard, M., Arnone, H. A., & Nemroff, D. (1986). Contextual influences on the post traumatic stress adaptation of homicide survivor victims, trauma and its wake. In

C. R. Figley (Ed.), *Traumatic stress theory research and intervention* (Vol. II). New York: Brunner/Mazel.

Bowlby, J. (1980). *Attachment and loss; Loss, sadness and depression, Vol. III.* New York: Basic Books.

Carter, W. B. (1971). Suicide, death and ghetto life. *Life & Threatening Behavior, 1,* 264-271.

Centers for Disease Control (CDC). (1987). Estimated years of potential life lost before age 65 and cause specific mortality by causes of death, United States, 1985. *MMWR, 36,* 811.

Danto, B. L., Brahns, J., & Kutscler, A. (1982). *The human side of homicide.* New York: Columbia University Press.

Engel, G. L. (1961). Is grief a disease? A challenge for medical research. *Psychosomatic Medicine, 23,* 18-22.

Gelles, R. (1974). *The violent home.* Beverly Hills: Sage.

Herjonic, M., & Meyer, D. (1976a). Notes on the epidemiology of homicide in an urban area. *Forensic Science, 8,* 235-245.

Holmes, T., & Masuda, M. (1978). Life changes and illness susceptibility. In B. S. Dohrenmend & B. P. Dohrenmend (Eds.), *Stress life events the nature and effects.* New York: John Wiley.

Kalish, D. K, & Reynolds, D. C. (1976). *Death and ethnicity: A pyschocultural study.* Farmingdale, NY: Baywood.

Kutash, I. L. (1978). Treating the victim of aggression and violence: Perspectives on murder and aggression. In I. L. Kutash, S. B. Kutash, & L. Schlesinger (Eds.), *Violence—Perspectives on murder and aggression* (pp. 446-461). San Francisco: Jossey-Bass.

Lidemann, E. (1944). The symptomology and management of acute grief. In E. Lidemann, *Beyond grief: Studies in crisis intervention* (pp. 60-78). New York: Jason Aronson.

MacIntosh, J. L., & Wrobleski, A. (1988). Grief reactions among suicide survivors an exploratory comparison of relationships, death studies, 12:21-39. Hemisphere.

Mendelsohn, B. A. (1956). A new branch of bio-psychosocial science: Victimology. *Revue Internationale de Criminologie et de Police Technique, 2,* 239-244.

Oxford English Dictionary. (1961). Volume XII.

Parker, C. M. (1972). *Bereavement: Studies of grief in adult life.* New York: International Universities Press.

Parker, C. M. (1976). The first year of bereavement: A longitudinal study of reaction of London widows to the death of their husbands. *Psychiatry, 33,* 444-467.

Stark, R., & McEvoy, J. (1970, November). Middle class violence. *Psychology Today,* 52-65.

U. S. Department of Health and Human Services. (1985). *Report of the secretary's task force on Black and minority health: Executive summary.* Washington, DC: Government Printing Office.

Von Hentig, H. (1947). *Crime: Causes and conditions.* New York: McGraw-Hill.

Wolfgang, M. E. (1970). *The sociology of crime and delinquency.* New York: John Wiley.

Worden, J. W. (1982). Resolving pathological grief. In *Grief counseling and grief therapy: A handbook for the mental health practitioner.* New York: Springer.

Author Index

Subject Index

About the Authors

Richard C. Cervantes received his Ph.D. in clinical psychology from Oklahoma State University in 1984. He served as research psychologist at the UCLA Spanish Speaking Mental Health Research Center, where he became involved in a series of research studies investigating stressful life events in the Hispanic community. He has published numerous articles on the mental health of Hispanics and has more recently developed a school-based prevention program for high-risk Hispanic youths. He currently is an Assistant Professor of Clinical Psychology at the University of Southern California School of Medicine and serves as supervising psychologist in the Division of Child and Adolescent Psychiatry.

Mario R. De La Rosa, Ph.D., is a social science analyst with the Epidemiologic Research Branch, National Institute on Drug Abuse. He received his doctorate in social welfare administration from The Ohio State University and his master's degree in social work from Case Western Reserve University. He currently manages a research grant portfolio on epidemiologic studies investigating the crime/drug connection and the drug use behavior of minority populations. He has been actively involved both in research on substance abuse in minority populations and in encouraging minority researchers to submit grants to NIDA. Before joining NIDA he was an assistant professor at the

University of Illinois at Urbana-Champaign. He is the author of several papers on social support systems of Hispanic individuals and reports on the crime/drug connection.

Christopher Fulton is a matriculating graduate student at California School of Professional Psychology, Los Angeles, in the Multicultural Community Clinical Proficiency. He received his undergraduate degree from California State University, Northridge. He spent a summer working with high-risk African-American adolescents in a city-funded community prevention program in Berkeley, California. For the past 2 years he has worked with gang members in a sub-acute psychiatric unit while on probation due to drug use or gang activity. He is currently doing research on achieving intercultural competence in clinical graduate programs. His dissertation interests lie in the area of the effects of white racial identity development on intercultural competence in counseling.

Tia Alane Nishimoto Hoffer received her Ph.D. in clinical psychology from the California School of Professional Psychology in 1991. For her dissertation Dr. Hoffer examined the effects of gang violence on Latino gang members and posttraumatic stress disorder as a viable diagnosis for this population. Currently, Dr. Hoffer is practicing at The H.E.L.P. Group as a therapist and coordinator of one of six residential treatment facilities for emotionally disturbed adolescents. Her professional interests involve multicultural community and clinical issues, women's issues, and the effects of violence and abuse as related to posttraumatic stress. Dr. Hoffer has participated in a national conference on gang violence as an assistant coordinator, and a conference on cultural diversity as a panelist.

Norma C. Johnson earned a bachelor's degree in political science from California State University, Dominguez Hills, and is currently working toward an M.S. in Criminal Justice at California State University, Long Beach. She was a Council Aide for Councilman David Cunningham for 5 years, then became a Victims Assistance Coordinator for the City Attorney's office in 1984. She founded a support group for families of homicide victims, and one year later the group became a counseling center, Loved Ones of Homicide Victims Service Center. Recognition for her work with victims and survivors of violent crime has brought her many awards, including the Governor's Victims Service Award, the

Director's Humanitarian Award from Charles Drew/Martin Luther King, Jr., Medical Center, and, most recently, the 1991 Citizen Awareness of the Law Award from the American Law Auxiliary.

Paul D. Juarez, Ph.D., is the Associate Director of the Primary Care Institute and Associate Professor of Family Medicine at the Charles R. Drew University of Medicine and Science in Los Angeles. Dr. Juarez has conducted several studies on victims of intentional injuries. He is also president of the board of directors of Loved Ones of Homicide Victims, a nonprofit organization in South Central Los Angeles that he co-founded. Dr. Juarez received his Ph.D. from the Florence Heller Graduate School for the Advanced Studies in Social Welfare at Brandeis University.

L. John Key, Ph.D. (Cand.), is co-founder and Executive Director of the Center Against Abusive Behavior. A graduate of California State University, Los Angeles, he is a doctoral candidate in clinical psychology at the California Graduate Institute, Los Angeles. He has spent the past 10 years providing evaluation and treatment in clinics, hospitals, and correctional facilities for people involved in abusive or assaultive behavior (physical, emotional, and sexual). He has also provided consultation and training to staff in the aforementioned facilities. He has made more than 100 presentations to professional organizations and has appeared on television and radio, speaking out against spousal abuse, including his appearance on the Black Entertainment Television program, "Family Violence in the Black Community."

Fred B. Martinez is currently assigned to the Gang Information Services Unit in the Parole Services Branch of the California Youth Authority, and has been with this entity since 1972. His primary duties include identifying and monitoring the movements of individuals involved in street gangs and prison gangs; evaluating gang-related data/information and disseminating such to affected agencies in California and the western states; providing consultation and technical assistance relative to gangs; serving as liaison to law enforcement agencies; establishing gang intelligence units and training; and apprehending missing parolees and/or escapees. He has been a trainer/instructor for numerous seminars on gangs and drugs to law enforcement, educational, and social services professionals; has made presentations at many conferences and universities; and has written a variety of articles on gang-related topics. He holds a B.A. in Corrections/Criminal Justice and an M.A. in Public Administration. He is a member of several gang task force groups and of the board of directors of Inland Behavioral Services, Inc.

Armando Morales, DSW, is Professor and Director of Clinical Social Work at the Neuropsychiatric Institute, UCLA School of Medicine, where he has been teaching since 1971. He is a former gang group worker and senior deputy probation officer, having worked with juvenile and adult forensic populations in the field and in institutions. Currently he is a mental health consultant and gang groups therapist with the California Youth Authority, and gang homicide prevention program and research consultant with the Kellogg Foundation and the Eisenhower Foundation. He has written extensively; his most recent book is the sixth edition of *Social Work: A Profession of Many Faces* (with Bradford W. Sheafor).

Lisa Porché-Burke is currently the Chancellor at the California School of Professional Psychology, Los Angeles, where she joined the faculty in 1985. She received her B.A. from the University of Southern California, and her Ph.D. and M.A. in counseling psychology with a specialization in ethnic minority issues from the University of Notre Dame. She has been a teacher and consultant for a number of years and has lectured extensively across the country and in Europe. She also remains active as an officer of the National Council of Schools of Professional Psychology (NCSPP)–Racial Ethnic Diversity Committee, APA Society for the Psychological Study of Ethnic Minority Issues, and Division of Psychotherapy on the Board of Ethnic Minority Affairs. Dr. Porché-Burke is dedicated to the promotion of mental health and well-being to underserved populations and to education around issues of diversity and multiculturalism. Her other publications include works for the American Psychological Association and in the *Journal of Counseling Psychology*.

Toshiaki Sasao received his Ph.D. in social psychology from the University of Southern California, and is a research psychologist in the Department of Psychology, University of California, Los Angeles. He was previously with the Institute for Health Promotion and Disease Prevention at the University of Southern California School of Medicine. He is also a program evaluator with several Asian/Pacific substance abuse prevention programs in the greater Los Angeles area. His current research focuses on the development of culturally anchored methodology for ethnic minority populations, especially in the area of substance abuse prevention. His other research interests include the application of social psychological principles to social issues, such as intergroup conflict reduction, the social influence approach to drug prevention in ethnic minority communities, social cognition in intergroup relations, telephone survey methodology, and multivariate techniques for categorical data.

Fernando I. Soriano, Ph.D., is a psychologist and currently an assistant professor in the Department of Behavioral Science at the University of Missouri, Kansas City. Prior to his university post, Dr. Soriano headed the U.S. Navy's in-house research project focused on assisting the development of support services to Navy families. He has conducted research and published in the areas of substance abuse, delinquency, AIDS, discrimination and mental health, cultural sensitivity, program design and evaluation. He is a consultant for many private and public agencies, and serves on several national committees, including the American Psychological Association's Committee on Youth Gang Drug Abuse Prevention for the Administration on Children, Youth, and Families. His book, *Conducting Needs Assessments: A Multidisciplinary Approach* will be published soon.

James Diego Vigil is Associate Professor at the University of Southern California. Dr. Vigil is a foremost expert in gang-related research, particularly with an emphasis on Latino gangs. He has published numerous research articles and books related to the issue of substance abuse and gang violence. Dr. Vigil serves on numerous local and national advisory committees relevant to gang violence prevention.

Saundrea D. Young received her MSW from the University of Michigan in 1973. A California Licensed Clinical Social Worker since 1978, she served as Assistant Director of Social Services at Martin Luther King, Jr., Hospital for 16 years, where she developed an expertise on the impact of emotional variables on physical recovery. In 1986 she co-founded the Loved Ones of Homicide Victims Service Center, where she is the Director of Clinical Services. She is currently the Assistant Department Administrator for Social Medicine at the Los Angeles Kaiser Permanente Medical Center. Her outstanding commitment to community service has been recognized with the May Company Outstanding Community Service Award, the Excellence in Service Award from the Charles Drew/Martin Luther King, Jr., Medical Center, and the American Cancer Society Community Service Award.

Al Wright is the Director of the Los Angeles County Office of Alcohol Programs. He is responsible for an annual budget of $40 million and a county-wide system of prevention and recovery services that brings him into contact with more than 125 community agencies. From 1980 to 1983, he was Alcohol Program Administrator of Alameda County. Mr. Wright has a B.A. and a J.D. from Louisiana State University.